HOW TO BE **EVANGELICAL**

WITHOUT BEING
CONSERVATIVE

::ROGER **E. OLSON**

HOW TO BE **EVANGELICAL**

WITHOUT BEING
CONSERVATIVE

ZONDERVAN®

ZONDERVAN.com/
AUTHORTRACKER
follow your favorite authors

ZONDERVAN®

How to Be Evangelical without Being Conservative
Copyright © 2008 by Roger E. Olson

Requests for information should be addressed to:
Zondervan, *Grand Rapids, Michigan* 49530

Library of Congress Cataloging-in-Publication Data

Olson, Roger E.
    How to be evangelical without being conservative / Roger E. Olson.
      p. cm.
    ISBN-10: 0-310-28338-8 (hardcover : alk. paper)
    ISBN-13: 978-0-310-28338-6 (hardcover : alk. paper)
    1. Evangelicalism. 2. Christian conservatism. 3. Conservatism. I. Title.
  BR1640.O47 2008
  270.8'3--dc22

                                 2007045560

Scripture taken from the *Revised Standard Version of the Bible,* copyright © 1946, 1952, 1971 by the Division of Christian Education of the National Council of Churches of Christ in the USA. Used by permission.

Internet addresses (websites, blogs, etc.) and telephone numbers printed in this book are offered as a resource to you. These are not intended in any way to be or imply an endorsement on the part of Zondervan, nor do we vouch for the content of these sites and numbers for the life of this book.

Interior design by Ben Fetterley

Printed in the United States of America

---

08 09 10 11 12 13 • 23 22 21 20 19 18 17 16 15 14 13 12 11 10 9 8 7 6 5 4 3 2 1

To Collin and Owen

CONTENTS

Foreword 9

Introduction:
*Who's an "Evangelical" and
What Does "Conservative" Mean?* 13

1. *Being Biblical without Orthodoxy* 29

2. *Building Character without Moralism* 43

3. *Celebrating America without Nationalism* 58

4. *Seeking Truth without Certainty* 73

5. *Taking the Bible Seriously without Literalism* 87

6. *Being Religionless without Secularism* 101

7. *Transforming Culture without Domination* 114

8. *Redistributing Wealth without Socialism* 128

9. *Relativizing without Rejecting Theology* 143

10. *Updating without Trivializing Worship* 157

11. *Accepting without Affirming Flawed People* 170

12. *Practicing Equality without Sacrificing Difference* 184

Conclusion:
Toward a Postconservative Evangelicalism 200

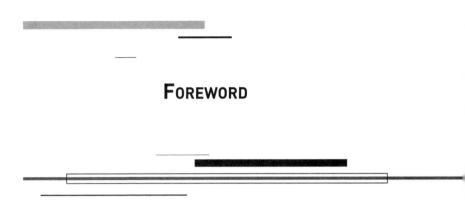

FOREWORD

Most of us are confronted daily with choices—choices to choose one thing or its apparent mirror opposite. What will we be? Catholic or Protestant, Democrat or Republican, Capitalist or Communist, Evangelical or Liberal, Emerging or Traditional, Moralist or Relativist, Seeker or Liturgical—we could go on but need not. Why? Nearly every mirror opposite you and I face presents a false dichotomy.

One of the more bewildering dichotomies of our day is the assumption, paraded daily in the media and on blogs and websites and by anyone who likes to sound off alarms, that Evangelical is opposed to Liberal in every way, shape, and form. Is it the case, many today are asking, that everything Evangelical is Conservative? Many of us are asking this question and are coming to surprising agreements on a variety of topics.

Roger Olson, in this splendidly clear and even-handed book, *How to be Evangelical without Being Conservative*, maps out an even dozen issues where the "more evangelical" line might just be a Third Way between being conservative or being liberal.

Let me give you a few reasons why I think you might like this book, because I sure did.

First, there are many Christians today who know deep inside they are neither conservative nor liberal on each issue. Some people, for good reasons, are liberal on one issue and conservative on another. Sometimes, however, we are neither liberal nor conservative — we are somewhere between the two. Standing between two mirror opposites is not always comfortable, but more often than not it is the best view available. It may not grab the media's attention, but it just might be right. There are all kinds of Christians who walk faithfully with our Lord who have found their way to a higher, middle ground. Olson shows that such a case is reasonable, and I hope lots of folks find the courage to take him at his word.

Second, the polarities of our political world today ruin genuine dialogue. When have you last seen a real socialist and a real capitalist sit down, side-by-side, and carry on a conversation about the most reasonable Christian understanding of the economy? You can bet it won't be on TV. Why? Because the stakes are too high. Because the lines in the sand have been drawn so deep that many who want to stand in the middle are afraid to step into the crossfire. Olson's book, so I think, will create an environment where dialogue can be invigorating for both sides and it will lead, so I hope, to some finding that a middle ground is firmer.

Third, the rhetoric of "who's right and who's not" has turned many seekers and good thinkers into pariahs. Those who happen to think that cherished doctrines deserve to be reexamined on the basis of the Bible are so quickly labeled "liberal" or "heretic" that the person who genuinely has questions runs into a corner. What happens to them? Because their faith is genuine and because they really do believe in the Bible but because in good conscience they have questions, they develop what can only be called an "ironic" faith. That is, they believe in the solid faith we've all come to love and know but they've got questions they can't ask, so they develop a "faith with questions." This irony weakens their confidence and their witness. Olson's book will encourage those previously labeled as pariahs to come out in the open and know that the items on the menu are more than two simple dishes.

Fourth, more of us need to be more humble about what we claim to be true. It is well and good to confess the Bible as the

Word of God. So it is. Our theology, which is—let's not forget this ever—*our attempt to put the Bible into our own categories*, is not the Word of God. This book reminds us that the two-option approach so popular in our world today, two options that are held with utter certitude by both sides, is not always the right one. Sometimes, in fact, there is a Third Way, a way that might not be so cocksure and certain, but just might be "Here I stand, so help me God."

Finally, the book you are holding in your hand right now is from a scholar who not only knows his stuff (my "technical" expression for a brilliant scholar) but who loves God and loves God's church. This book is not some highbrow book designed to prove how much a scholar knows. This book is for anyone who knows that deep inside there are often middle ways, a Third Way, another option—one that gets beyond the polarities and finds common ground that both sides are neglecting.

Bless you, Roger, for this fine book.

Scot McKnight
Karl A. Olsson Professor in Religious Studies,
North Park University, Chicago, Illinois

WHO'S AN "EVANGELICAL" AND WHAT DOES "CONSERVATIVE" MEAN?

As long as I can remember I've considered myself *both* "evangelical" *and* "an evangelical." As an adjective, "evangelical" means being committed to the gospel of Jesus Christ, which is supposed to be good news. To me, it always has been unqualified, unconditional good news—that Jesus Christ shows the loving heart of God by dying on the cross so that sinful men and women can be saved and enjoy a relationship with God now and into eternity. As a noun "evangelical" means a person who belongs to a large and diverse community of people who are similarly committed to the good news of Jesus Christ.

Of course, there's more to being evangelical than that, but the gospel lies at the core of the matter. After all the wrangling over who is truly "evangelical" and "an evangelical," I'm tempted to say "anyone is an evangelical who is sincerely, passionately committed to the gospel of Jesus Christ as that is conveyed to us through the inspired narratives of the Bible." Another way of putting it is that anyone is an evangelical who is a God-fearing, Bible-believing, Jesus-loving Christian. I know that won't satisfy some people who want the label evangelical to mean more, but I've become satisfied with this broad definition.

Shifting Evangelical Labels

I used to think of myself as a "conservative Christian," though I never thought of myself as a "fundamentalist." Let me explain. In my past "conservative Christian" was part of being evangelical; if a person was committed to the gospel of Jesus Christ, she was expected to take a generally traditional approach to interpreting the Bible and confessing Christian doctrines. A fundamentalist, on the other hand, was someone who elevated minor Christian beliefs and matters of opinion to the status of dogmas and defended them militantly against all "compromises" with secularity and liberal thinking. Especially after World War II, fundamentalists were those conservative Christians who considered Billy Graham dangerously liberal because he welcomed Roman Catholics and mainline Protestants to cooperate in his evangelistic crusades. Other conservative Christians, however, were simply evangelicals who embraced the ministry of Billy Graham and tended to be somewhat more relaxed in their attitudes toward doctrine and ecumenical cooperation than were fundamentalists.

I learned these categories (evangelical, conservative, fundamentalist) in college and seminary and held onto them for many years. They served me well as I attempted to categorize and describe the blooming, buzzing confusion of American Christianity.

Let me illustrate. I grew up participating in a large, interdenominational organization called Youth for Christ. There I rubbed shoulders with fellow students of many Protestant denominations and even a few Roman Catholics. We shared a common commitment to the gospel of Jesus Christ and were all passionate about having a "personal relationship" with him, which included "quiet times" (daily devotions), Bible study, regular worship, and "witnessing" (sharing the gospel with others and inviting them to be saved). We were all evangelicals and, for the most part, conservative in our beliefs and morals. We didn't talk about politics or social issues; we focused exclusively on evangelism, worship, devotions, and fun. We strictly avoided those relatively minor doctrinal differences that separated our denominations—such as whether Jesus Christ would return before, during, or after the so-called "tribulation" and the proper way to baptize people. Well, we may have discussed such issues, but we never expected everyone to believe the same about them.

Being evangelical was important to us; we valued our evangelical identity because it set us apart from "nominal Christians"—those who didn't take their faith seriously or allow it to affect their daily lives. Nominal Christians merely attended some church occasionally and considered themselves Christians because of some formal association with a Christian church. We evangelicals sought a "higher life" of intense personal faith and commitment to Jesus Christ.

But as much as we disparaged nominal Christians and tried to "win them to the Lord," we also knew the difference between ourselves and the "fundamentalists" in our town. They shared many of our beliefs and commitments, but they wouldn't have anything to do with us because we were, to them, polluted by our "compromised Christianity." Some of us went to movies, we didn't adhere strictly or militantly enough to what they considered a literal interpretation of the whole Bible, and we had Christian fellowship with believers of all denominations, including Catholics.

The fundamentalists were our "evangelical fringe"—the evangelicals who were always mad at someone. They puzzled and bewildered us. When an associate evangelist of Billy Graham came to our town to hold an evangelistic crusade, the fundamentalists and mainline Christians didn't cooperate even if some of them snuck in to listen. The fundamentalists considered Billy Graham too liberal; the mainliners considered him too conservative if not fundamentalist! We thought we were just right because we were in the middle. We loved Billy Graham and looked to him as our model of being authentically evangelical because of his clear commitment to the Bible and to the gospel of Jesus Christ without narrowness, rigidity, or anger.

So, I grew up well into my mature years interpreting the Christian world around me using these three general categories:

fundamentalists to the far right, mainline Christians to the left, and evangelicals in the middle. And we thought we were the perfect conservative Christians. Yes, the fundamentalists were conservative also, but theirs was a "maximal conservatism" that made us cringe as they, for example, rejected modern Bible translations and insisted that only the King James Version of the Bible is inspired and authoritative. Anything new they rejected, and they specialized in condemning fellow Christians for their role in the things noted above.

If you had asked me in the 1970s whether being evangelical and being conservative were inextricably linked, I would have considered the question odd. How could they be separated? So long as we weren't excessive in our conservatism by being militant, angry, too narrow, or rigid, I gladly accepted the label "conservative Christian" and even "conservative evangelical." Being conservative simply meant taking the Bible seriously as God's inspired, written Word, believing in Jesus Christ as God and Savior, being generally respectful toward traditional Christian doctrines such as the Trinity (even if you didn't know what they meant), and living by "biblical moral standards" such as the Ten Commandments. We debated "matters of conviction" (individual conscience) such as smoking and going to movies, but they weren't litmus tests of being authentically Christian.

Throughout the 1980s and 1990s, however, the labels and categories I've been describing started changing and became more problematic for me and for many other Christians. One major reason was the national news media's varying and sometimes unpredictable uses of them. Many of my friends and acquaintances no longer call themselves evangelical because they consider that term hopelessly linked forever with the so-called "Religious Right"—a movement of ultra-conservative, mostly fundamentalist Christians who use politics to dominate American social life with their blend of social and religious conservatism. This began in the late 1970s with the rise of fundamentalist leader Jerry Falwell to prominence as a religious and political force to be reckoned with. He and others founded the Moral Majority in an attempt to use government to promote what they considered conservative morality.

Falwell and people like him managed to garner the media's attention as they touted themselves as the true spokesmen for "evangelical Christianity" in America. The irony is that in the 1960s Falwell was one of those rigid, narrow, militant fundamentalists preaching on the fringes of the larger, more diverse evangelical community. At that time he eschewed the label "evangelical" and criticized leading evangelicals for being too broad and inclusive. But during the 1980s and 1990s he reinvented himself and managed to make himself and people like him the media standards of evangelicalism. Even more impressive was the way these fundamentalists claimed and cornered the label "conservative Christian" (or "Christian conservative") for themselves.

Separating "Evangelical" from "Conservative"

Gradually the impression has sunk into the American mind that being a conservative Christian, being evangelical, and being narrow, rigid, militant, and angry are the same. But more important, the media's use of these terms and categories has left the impression on the public mind that being evangelical means having a knee-jerk reaction against any and every cause considered progressive or liberal. During the 1800s there was a saying in Great Britain that the Church of England was the Tory Party (conservative party) at prayer. During the 1990s and into the twenty-first century many people feel that the Republican Party, now controlled by people who would probably have been considered ultra-conservatives in the 1960s and 1970s, is the evangelical Christian party and that evangelical churches are simply the Republican Party at prayer.

Because of this popular linkage in the media, many of my friends and acquaintances (and more than a few of my students and colleagues in traditionally evangelical universities and seminaries) have found it difficult to hold onto the label "evangelical." They want to put a distance between themselves and the Religious

Right, and the only way they know to do that is to stop calling themselves (or allowing themselves to be called) evangelical. But they don't know what new label to use to distinguish themselves from other Christians such as fundamentalists and mainline, liberal Protestants (who often seem to consider themselves the Democratic Party at prayer!). Being simply "Christian" would be nice, but it doesn't work because of the extreme diversity of Christianity in America. "What kind of Christian are you?" is the unavoidable question. Mentioning a denomination doesn't help much because either people haven't heard of it (or know little about it) or it is so diverse as to include almost anything and everything. To my friends who want to drop the label evangelical I ask, "What label do you prefer?"

I still consider myself evangelical and an evangelical. My theology is consistent with historic evangelical Christianity and I locate myself gladly within the larger evangelical Christian community. But I feel the pain of those who chafe at the label because it lands them alongside the ultra-conservative advocates of the Religious Right and/or fundamentalists. Many of us find ourselves in a quandary: how to rescue the label "evangelical" in this culture where it is so widely considered just another word for "conservative Christian" and where that label is generally identified with fundamentalism and the Religious Right.

That is the issue I hope to answer in this book. My purpose is to explain how a person can be evangelical and not conservative, let alone fundamentalist, *in the contemporary sense of that term.* I believe it is not too late to salvage the label "evangelical," but I think it is too late and simply unnecessary (if not wrong) to identify that with being conservative. Just as my parents and grandparents fought to rescue their evangelical identity from fundamentalism, so I want to rescue it from conservatism.

So who really is an evangelical? Who is a fundamentalist? What does it mean to be conservative as a Christian? The plain fact is that these are shifting categories and terms in dispute. They are essentially contested concepts. They don't work as absolute descriptors. The media have contributed to their elasticity by calling fundamentalist leaders like Jerry Falwell evangelicals and moderate evangelicals like C. S. Lewis fundamentalists. (I have actually seen articles in secular publications calling Lewis an Anglican fundamentalist!)

In other words, I intend to challenge one major, almost undisputed category. Most people assume that to be evangelical is to be conservative socially, politically, and theologically. The label "conservative evangelical" seems like a tautology (a case of unnecessary repetition). Aren't all evangelical Christians conservative even if not fundamentalists? In a day and time when the old division between fundamentalism and evangelicalism is breaking down, I want to suggest that authentic evangelicalism is not even necessarily conservative (let alone fundamentalist). But I admit up front that all these terms and categories, labels and concepts are fluid and relative. None of them has an absolute meaning. Each is tied to some context and slips away when the phenomenon being described is viewed from a different angle.

What was Jerry Falwell? He called himself a fundamentalist and then an evangelical; he was treated as a spokesman for conservative Christians and evangelicals generally by the media. What is Billy Graham? He's criticized by some fundamentalists as liberal, but his own beliefs are conservative overall. Real liberals consider him (along with C. S. Lewis) a fundamentalist! In all this confusion many religious leaders and scholars have settled on one label as most useful: conservative evangelical. It seems to describe many fundamentalists and evangelicals well and many of them gladly embrace it for themselves. That worries me.

It worries me because words use us as much as we use words. Although the label conservative has no absolute meaning, it tends to signal a certain stance with regard to the past and tradition. It enshrines them as sacred. I find the juxtaposition of conservative (in that sense) and evangelical (in my sense, at least) filled with tension. I gladly call myself evangelical in a time when many who think and live like me are dropping it as useless or worse. It has come to be so closely associated with the likes of Jerry Falwell and others of the Religious Right in America that many who are not so conservative find it problematic. I am not able to discard the label evangelical even though I wear it at times uncomfortably. By contrast, I am not so dedicated to the label "conservative" and even feel that it contradicts the true spirit of being evangelical in the best sense.

This sense of tension between "evangelical" and "conservative" first hit me during a potluck dinner at church. I was sitting across from the wife of a retired Baptist minister. She and her husband were most certainly not fundamentalists of the militant style. But in response to an unremembered comment nearby she declared most emphatically, "But we are a conservative people, you know." I heard myself say, "I'm not so sure we should be." I wasn't certain what I meant, so I couldn't adequately explain to her and others around the table why I said that. Later my reasoning became clearer to me: "conservative" sounds defensive of the past and the status quo. Even some dictionaries define it that way. "Evangelical" sounds both radical and open to new things. Not open to anything and everything, of course, but willing to venture out of comfort zones and risk vested interests for the sake of the gospel and biblical fidelity.

Let me explain. If I heard a fellow evangelical declare among a group of real theological liberals who deny the supernatural inspiration of the Bible, "We are a conservative people, you know," I'd probably agree with her. Context matters. In a room full of Christians who are more than open to anything and everything new and who question all the doctrines so hard won by the church fathers and Reformers, I'd identify as conservative. But I rarely find myself in such contexts.

In a room full of evangelicals, however, I am reluctant to identify as conservative because that only reinforces the already prevailing pull of our fundamentalist past and the tug of resurgent fundamentalism among us. It also tends to quench the spirit of forward, progressive, and radically biblical thinking and living. It usually means favoritism toward what has always been thought and done by us; it usually signals a knee-jerk negative reaction to anything innovative, creative, and progressive even if it is thoroughly biblical, God-honoring, and Jesus-glorifying. And, of course, it tends to identify one as a sympathizer with, if not participant in, the Religious Right in America. I would like to suggest that it is possible to be more evangelical by being less conservative in the sense of "conservative" just described. That's because to me "evangelical" means being radically open to the gospel in all of its implications, including challenges to our comfort zones and vested interest in upholding the status quo and reiterating the past. To my understanding "evangelical" includes placing the cross of Jesus Christ over and above all our precious previous thinking and being ready and willing to think again. The cross relativizes our traditions. It condemns all idolatry—including worship of the past, of institutions, of comfort zones. It calls us to die to all of that and take risks for God. That's not conservative or liberal; it's radical, extreme, and progressive.

Radical Evangelical History

"Liberal" in today's marketplace of ideas means accommodation to the spirit of the modern or postmodern age. That's why liberal churches are dying; they are little more than clubs to reinforce Enlightenment-based thinking and living. Most people know intuitively that Christianity must be more than that. But Christianity is also more than conservation of traditions, including "the American way." Were the early Christians conservative? Even a quick reading of the book of Acts in the New Testament or the writings of the second-century church fathers will disabuse anyone of that notion! So why should twenty-first-century Christians be conservative? Linking conservative and evangelical in the way many people do tends to suggest that evangelicals take a defensive posture toward values and habits and customs of the past. Is that why twentieth-century evangelicals were notoriously slow to embrace movements for social justice in contrast to their nineteenth-century counterparts?

Even a cursory study of evangelical history reveals that nineteenth-century evangelicals were not conservative. They rejected the majority liberalism and dead orthodoxy of the mainline churches in favor of radical conversion and transformation of life. That flowed over into their social attitudes. In England a leading evangelical named William Wilberforce led the movement to abolish the slave trade in Great Britain and its empire. In the United States evangelical evangelist and college president Charles Finney was a radical abolitionist who also advocated for full equality of women in society and churches.

As another example, B. T. Roberts was a Methodist who founded a new denomination called the Free Methodist Church, which still exists. He was a social progressive who promoted redistribution of wealth through social mechanisms such as inheritance tax. In fact, he was the first person to suggest it. Roberts also eliminated the practice of renting church pews (whence the "Free" in Free Methodist). Moreover, he believed in the full equality of women, including ordination of women to be pastors of churches. The Free Methodist Church was the first Christian denomination to ordain women and it was most definitely evangelical. The story of radical Christianity among nineteenth-century evangelicals has already been told by scholars such as Timothy Smith and Donald W. Dayton (*Rediscovering an Evangelical Heritage* [Harper & Row, 1976]). Experiments in nonconservative, progressive evangelicalism have gained some notice in the media, but they have generally been treated as something less than authentically evangelical or as quirky and marginal.

Most notable of all exceptions to the rule that all evangelicals are socially and politically conservative as well as traditionalist is the Sojourners community in Washington, D.C., which publishes *Sojourners* magazine (earlier called *The Post-American*). Its leader, Jim Wallis, occasionally appears on television talk shows as the poster child for an anomaly of nonconservative evangelicalism. Koinonia Farms in Americus, Georgia, is another experiment in postconservative evangelical life, a group where racially integrated evangelical Christians work together to fight poverty. Among theologians, a group of postmodern evangelicals has become controversial for rejecting conservatism in favor of radical Christian faith. Among them are Clark Pinnock, Stanley Grenz (now deceased), Henry Knight, John Franke, and John Sanders. The focus of this network is the Evangelical Theology Group of the American Academy of Religion.

My point is that nonconservative, or what I prefer to call postconservative, evangelicalism has a history; it is not something I'm advocating for the first time. I explained it in detail in *Reformed and Always Reforming: The Postconservative Approach to Evangelical Theology* (Baker Academic, 2007). My intent here is to show readers the way forward with postconservative evangelicalism. How is it possible now to be both authentically evangelical and nonconservative or postconservative?

On Being Postconservative without Being Postevangelical

Before I launch into that project, however, I ought to explain further what I mean by evangelical. Why am I so reluctant to give up that label? Why not simply opt for being postevangelical? Isn't the attempt to disentangle "conservative" and "evangelical" a Quixotic campaign like the famous Don of fiction jousting at windmills? I hope not. I think there are enough people out there who fit the mold of authentic evangelical faith that there is hope for the concept; I want to rescue it from the hands of those who would fold it into being conservative and to breathe new life into it.

So what do I mean by evangelical? I've tried to describe that in some other books I've written. If you want a fuller account than is possible here, I suggest you look at my *The Westminster Handbook to Evangelical Theology* (Westminster John Knox, 2005) or the smaller *The Pocket History of Evangelical Theology* (InterVarsity Press, 2007). Both focus on theology and doctrine; in this book I want to expand that to social attitudes and habits of the mind and heart. I will argue that it is possible to be more evangelical by being less conservative in these habits and attitudes.

By evangelical I still mean what I meant in the books mentioned above. And I mean what is meant by most scholars of evangelicalism minus the frequent element of social, political, and theological conservatism. Evangelicals are mostly Protestant Christians who display four characteristics: *biblicism* (belief in the supreme authority of Scripture for faith and life), *conversionism* (belief that authentic Christianity always includes a radical conversion to Jesus Christ by personal repentance and faith that begins a lifelong personal relationship with him), *crucicentrism* (piety, devotional life, and worship centered around the cross of Jesus Christ), and *activism* (concern for and involvement in social transformation through evangelism and social action).

These are the four hallmarks of authentic evangelicalism identified by evangelical historians David Bebbington and Mark Noll, and they have achieved almost canonical status among evangelical scholars and scholars of evangelicalism. (See Bebbington and Noll's book *Evangelicalism: Studies in Popular Protestantism in North America, the British Isles and Beyond, 1700–1990* [Oxford University Press, 1994].) I will be referring to these hallmarks, plus one more, throughout this book. That added hallmark is *respect for the Great Tradition of Christian doctrine.*

Have I just turned back toward conservatism as a hallmark of authentic evangelicalism? I don't think so. First of all, by "respect" I do not mean slavish adherence. All thinking evangelicals are generally respectful of the achievements of the church fathers and the Reformers in terms of carving out the major doctrines of Christianity. Second, in today's church culture being respectful of Christian doctrines as they have been hard won by the church fathers and Reformers goes against the status quo insofar as that is reflected in a popular folk religion. Folk Christianity often emphasizes finding happiness and fulfillment in Jesus Christ without the cross or doctrine. I am an evangelical in the sense of all five hallmarks together—and so are most or all evangelicals whether they identify themselves as conservative or not.

Another way of explaining who's an evangelical is to say we all respect and admire Billy Graham. It sounds less than scholarly to say so! But, in fact, I've been in scholarly meetings where experts were trying to pin down a common evangelical identity and finally agreed that it comes down to admiration for Billy Graham. Of course, that is only a contemporary definition of this religious phenomenon. It doesn't work for past evangelicals or future ones. But it does seem that today, in 2007, the label evangelical is shared by people who admire Billy Graham and think his preaching is true while those who are not so enamored with him and his message tend not to call themselves evangelicals. I am an evangelical in both senses, sharing the four historical and social hallmarks described by Bebbington and Noll (to which I have added a fifth) and admiration of Billy Graham.

So, in short and in essence, my claim is that being evangelical is not so much a matter of adherence to a set of doctrines, although evangelicals are generally respectful of the basic doctrines of Christianity, as it is of a matter of an experience and a spirituality centered around the Bible, Jesus Christ and his cross, and conversion, devotion, and evangelism. Likewise, "conservative" is not so much a matter of adherence to a list of causes as it is a habit of the heart. Conservatism values tradition and tends to be suspicious of anything that goes against tradition. What constitutes tradition depends on the context, of course, but conservatism is protecting and defending perceived traditional values, beliefs, and practices.

Yes, in today's society, because of the media, conservatism also tends to mean sympathy for, if not active promotion of, the causes of political and social conservatives. To many people it means favoring small government and states' rights. And it may also mean opposing abortion and homosexual marriages. The media has created a list of such "conservative causes." My use of "conservative" here, however, is not like that even though I acknowledge that use as legitimate and probably inescapable. When I claim that it is possible to be more evangelical by being less conservative, I mean by "conservative" that habit of the heart that reacts against anything nontraditional and tends toward an idolatry of some perceived past "golden age" when church and society were good and not yet corrupted by forces of secularity and liberal thinking.

Similarly, by "evangelical" I mean a religious and spiritual habit of the heart that values having a healthy, growing, personal relationship with Jesus Christ manifested in a "conversional piety." Conversional piety is the network of interrelated beliefs and practices that include repentance and faith in Jesus Christ as God, Lord, and Savior; commitment to the Bible as God's inspired, written Word as uniquely authoritative for Christian life and practice; daily devotions and regular worship and Bible study; cross-centered devotion that regards Jesus' death on the cross as the turning point of history and personal life; and active participation in social transformation through evangelism and charitable caring for the poor and oppressed.

Of course, not everyone will agree with my delineations of "conservative" and "evangelical" here. However, I think they are broad enough to ring a bell with most people who have ever considered what these labels mean. And I think most people will recognize how intimately connected they have become in contemporary American social, political, and religious life. To a certain extent, they have been connected for most of the twentieth century. But this was not always so — and it doesn't need to be so today. I hope that as we progress into the twenty-first century more and more people will consider the possibility of being evangelical without being conservative. Here I want to map out the way forward for those of us who want to be evangelical and wish to continue using that label for ourselves without being considered conservative or wearing that label.

In the process what will become apparent, I hope, is my desire to disengage being evangelical from any particular social or political ideology, party, or platform. To a great extent people in the early twenty-first century consider evangelicalism a conservative political movement as well as a conservative spiritual and religious one. Others have already challenged that. I want to go beyond that to even challenging the idea that being evangelical includes a conservative habit of the heart. Not only should we as evangelicals eschew any close relationship with a political movement or list of causes; we should also avoid a backward-looking, traditionalist approach to discovering the good, the true, and the beautiful. We should become more open to finding those in the new, the innovative and creative, the radical and cutting edge. Evangelicalism should be an "edgy" religious and spiritual attitude and habit of the heart. As an evangelical I think I should be open to risk without throwing the baby out with the bathwater. I don't want to discard everything of the past, but being radically biblical is more important to me than being orthodox or traditional. I think many evangelicals share that vision with me. It is for them that I write.

CHAPTER 1

BEING BIBLICAL WITHOUT ORTHODOXY

Every year I take a class of students to visit an Eastern Orthodox worship service. We are mostly Baptists, so we sit, stand,
observe, and listen, but we don't participate. That's because we're
not Orthodox; even the priest of the Greek Orthodox church we
visit lets us know in a most friendly way that, while we are welcome there, we are not there to partake of the Eucharist (Lord's
Supper). We're not Orthodox *or* orthodox in their eyes. In fact,
to them our churches are not even really churches; they are "religious clubs" or parachurch organizations. The priest is quick to
explain that he doesn't mean we're not saved. That's God's business, and he assumes people who have repented and believed in
Jesus Christ are saved, but the church of Jesus Christ is identical
with the fellowship of churches under Eastern Orthodox bishops. Many Orthodox Christians would now include the churches
under the pope — the bishop of Rome (Catholics).

The Many Meanings of Orthodoxy

I used to explain to my students that we Baptists and other evangelical Christians think we're the truly orthodox Christians.
I enjoyed the irony that this other fellowship of churches from
Eastern Europe and the Middle East call themselves "Orthodox"
while we are really more orthodox than they are! This play on
words is confusing, so let me explain.

In religious jargon "orthodox" may simply mean "theologically correct." You've heard of "politically correct." Well, orthodoxy with a small "o" is simply theological correctness. Every branch of Christianity thinks it is more orthodox than others; otherwise there would be little reason for existing as a separate denomination. The Eastern Orthodox family of churches has long embraced and used the "O" label because they highly value being theologically correct; to them it is of greatest importance after right worship, which is also part of being orthodox in their eyes. They affirm the ancient creeds of Christendom, such as the Nicene Creed, and repeat them often. And they seek to adhere to the teachings of the church fathers of the first eight centuries. As one Eastern Orthodox priest told us, "All important questions were answered in the first eight centuries" — by the church fathers and the ecumenical (universal) councils of the church.

Traditionally, then, religious scholars use "Orthodox" with a capital "O" to refer to that family of churches looking to the ancient church fathers and councils of the first seven or eight centuries and in submission to the great patriarchs of the ancient capital cities of Christendom (e.g., the Patriarch of Constantinople, a city in Turkey now called Istanbul). We often use "orthodox" with a small "o" to designate theological correctness. The first use is descriptive whereas the second one is prescriptive. To adherents of Eastern Orthodoxy, of course, the two are the same.

There's another, less scholarly but more popular meaning of "orthodoxy" I use in this chapter. In popular parlance orthodoxy means being locked into tradition and closed to new ways of thinking, living, believing, worshiping, and practicing the Christian faith. An orthodox Christian, in this sense, is any Christian who stands firmly for tradition — however that is perceived. But orthodoxy in this sense especially relates to doctrine; orthodoxy is firm and unwavering adherence to a set of doctrines that are usually expressed in some creed and/or confessional statement. In other words, it is more than just "theological correctness" because everyone who thinks about God would like to be theologically correct. Theological correctness is an ideal identical with right thinking. We all want to think we think rightly.

The sense of orthodoxy I'm talking about now is more that just thinking rightly because it enshrines a particular set of doctrines carved out of Scripture, tradition, reason, and experience (the so-called Wesleyan Quadrilateral) and carved into stone at some time in the past by some group of people. The people who defined this orthodox set of doctrines may be bishops (as in Roman Catholic councils) or ministers or theologians (as in many Protestant denominations). In this sense, orthodoxy is affirming allegiance without mental reservation or qualification to these traditional beliefs.

The word "orthodoxy," then, has three distinct connotations: (1) that family of churches in submission to a group of patriarchs (super-bishops) of Eastern Europe and the Middle East called Eastern Orthodoxy, (2) theological correctness as an ideal, and (3) strict adherence to and affirmation of a formal set of doctrines expressed in written creeds and confessions of faith. For members of Eastern Orthodoxy, of course, all three are identical. The Roman Catholic Church also rolls them into one with the exception that it considers only the churches under the bishop of Rome (the pope) completely orthodox. Protestants have a special problem with orthodoxy number three because Martin Luther and other sixteenth-century Reformers rebelled against that orthodoxy. When Luther was asked to recant his beliefs such as that salvation is by God's grace through faith alone and not through faith and good works, he appealed to God's Word (the Bible) and reason against popes and church councils (i.e., against a magisterium of orthodoxy) and said they contradicted each other. In other words, he appealed to Scripture and reason against orthodoxy itself.

The Protestant Principle

Beginning with Luther, all Protestants have always affirmed *sola scriptura* (Scripture alone) as the test of true belief. This was radical stuff in Luther's time. One hundred years earlier the Bohemian reformer John Hus was burned at the stake for the same rebellious attitude toward official orthodoxy. Of course, both

Luther and Hus wanted to be orthodox in the sense of theologically correct. But neither one wanted to bow down and accept without question traditional beliefs that could not be proved by Scripture and that went against reason. They were against being orthodox in that sense.

Later, however, successive generations of Protestants began to forget the value of checking every Christian belief, however ancient and widely accepted or enforced by an inquisition, by Scripture. They began to develop statements of faith that took on the aura of authority reminiscent of the Catholic Church's creeds. Luther's followers first wrote the Augsburg Confession as a statement of faith to show the Holy Roman Emperor that they were theologically correct according to Scripture. Later that same confession came to be treated as an inviolable and incorrigible creed by some conservative Lutherans.

Now there's irony. John Calvin, the Reformer of Switzerland and especially Geneva, the great organizer of Protestant thought, had "heretic" Michael Servetus burned at the stake for his refusal to accept orthodox doctrines. Catholics and Protestants alike hunted down and killed Anabaptists because they wouldn't conform to belief in infant baptism and insisted on baptizing adults only. They were killed for rejecting the orthodoxy of their day, which was shared by both Protestants and Catholics. Many Anabaptists also rejected the detailed, formal systems of doctrine developed by their fellow Protestants.

Protestants have always claimed to believe in Scripture above tradition; every doctrine is to be tested by Scripture and whatever cannot be proven by Scripture is not to be preached or taught as true. Of course, people may be free to hold opinions, but official teachings of the churches should be clearly biblical and not merely traditional. That's the meaning of *sola scriptura* — not Scripture as the only book to read but Scripture as the ultimate source and standard of truth especially for Christian faith and practice. However, many Protestants have faltered at this and insisted that people in their churches simply affirm doctrines without asking whether they are biblical or challenging them by Scripture.

Conservative Presbyterians have the Westminster Confession of Faith; conservative Dutch Reformed have the Canons and Decrees of the Synod of Dort (1618/1619). At that synod or council of Reformed "divines" (ministers and theologians), a group of Dutch dissenters known as the Remonstrants (which really means the same as "Protestants") were tried as heretics because they were judged to have departed from the traditional doctrines of the Reformed churches of Europe. Their leader had been Jacob Arminius (d. 1609), who was widely acknowledged to be a brilliant biblical scholar and theologian of his day. He taught theology at the University of Leyden in the Netherlands and rejected the doctrines of absolute, unconditional predestination in favor of belief in free will and human cooperation with God's grace in salvation. His followers, the Remonstrants, came to be called Arminians. The Reformed delegates to the Synod of Dort judged them harshly for rejecting what was considered traditional belief in God's absolute sovereignty, and they were stripped of their positions and property and exiled from the Netherlands. One was beheaded—all this in the name of orthodoxy.

Of course, later, the Remonstrants and Arminians developed their own official versions of orthodoxy and in some cases expelled people who disagreed even if they marshaled biblical arguments for their views. This is the natural human tendency—"hardening of the categories." As radical denominations seeking freedom from religious oppression at the hands of gatekeepers of orthodoxy become older and more established, they tend to create and enforce their own orthodoxies and oppress free thinkers who dare to challenge them.

Orthodoxy in this sense, then, is enforced adherence to a written doctrinal system under threat of punishment for daring to question it. Of course, not everyone who affirms this orthodoxy is doing so under threat of punishment (such as excommunication). Many gladly affirm orthodoxy without reservation. Others, however, find it imperative to question orthodoxies of this kind (written, formal, enforced) in order to keep the churches "reformed and always reforming." That was also a major Protestant principle: *reformata et semper reformanda* — "reformed and always reforming."

The Reformers let a genie out of the bottle; they opened a can of worms. Once the value of questioning orthodoxy and testing it by Scripture caught on, it couldn't be stopped. It turned back against Protestant orthodoxies with harsh consequences. How ironic it is that Protestants punished people for daring to question or protest formal human doctrines by appealing to Scripture. That's exactly what Luther did and why he's considered a hero. But don't dare to challenge anything in the Lutheran *Book of Concord* (the set of official doctrinal statements and standards of Lutherans worldwide)! What would Luther say?

Doctrine without Orthodoxy

Most younger Christians today (with notable exceptions) are weary of orthodoxy; the postmodern culture and mindset encourage questioning everything. Dangle a proposition labeled "orthodox" in front of most postmodern people, including Christians, and you simply dare them to challenge it. That's especially true if its only justification is that it is traditional: "We've always believed this, so you must believe it also." It's like waving a red flag in front of a bull; today's young Christians by and large have caught the spirit of Luther. They want to know if a doctrine is scriptural and reasonable before they affirm it. And if they aren't convinced, they want to ponder it and maybe even reject it — or hold it in suspension until more evidence for or against it comes along.

This seemingly cavalier attitude toward orthodoxy among the young frightens and shocks some conservative evangelical leaders. They notice it especially among the "emerging church" crowd — those mostly young Christians who experiment with new ways of worshiping, believing, and being church using postmodern cultural norms. Some conservative evangelical spokesmen have lashed out against these inquiring minds who dare to question traditional orthodoxy. Of course, insofar as they are denying orthodox beliefs on the basis of some extrabiblical authority such as philosophy or culture, all evangelicals will be dismayed. Not because they are daring to question but because they are abandoning the source and norm that makes Christians Christian—God's Word. People are free to reject that Word, but then they abdicate the right to call themselves Christians. The problem is, however, that many critics of the young and restless, mostly postmodern emerging church Christians are criticizing them merely for doubting and challenging orthodox beliefs and practices.

My proposal is that orthodoxy is never sacrosanct; it is always "man-made" and never delivered directly from God's mouth or hands. Doctrines are the product of theological reflection at best based on faithful reflection on God's Word. Secondary sources and norms such as tradition, reason, and experience come into play in the construction of orthodoxy, but they are not equal in authority with the Bible itself. Conservative evangelicals tend to use some tradition such as Calvinism or Arminianism as the indispensable standard of correct interpretation of the Bible. Then those traditions become equal in authority with the Bible. Some younger, postmodern Christians fall into the trap of discarding everything traditional using postmodern culture or their own experience as the ultimate touchstone of truth. But, in any case, insofar as we have doctrines or even an orthodoxy of being against doctrines, these are human inventions and never divinely inspired. That insight lies at the root of Protestantism itself, and it is necessary for the continual reform of the churches.

If I am right, then it is the most natural thing in the world for faithful Christians to question and challenge orthodoxy in light of Scripture. All Protestants pay at least lip service to Scripture over tradition, but their real convictions are revealed in how they treat traditional doctrinal statements such as creeds and written statements of faith. Some require candidates for ministerial ordination and other church leaders to pledge allegiance to creeds and confessions of faith. Some conservative Reformed churches, for example, require candidates to affirm the Heidelberg Catechism, the Belgic Confession of Faith, and the Canons and Decrees of the Synod of Dort without mental reservation. If they later develop mental reservations about them, they are supposed to register those with the proper church authorities. At least one Pentecostal denomination annually sends out a questionnaire to all ordained and licensed ministers asking them to reaffirm five traditional Pentecostal beliefs. Anyone who neglects or refuses to do it is immediately investigated for possible heresy.

My question in this chapter is whether it is possible to be authentically evangelical without being orthodox *in this sense of the word*. Can a person be truly evangelical in the sense explained in the introduction without affirming doctrines without mental reservation or even while challenging traditional beliefs and practices using faithful and fresh biblical investigation and interpretation as the source and norm? I believe it is possible. That doesn't mean that I allow anything and everything to be compatible with evangelical faith. By no means! Evangelical faith is rooted and grounded in the soil of biblicism; all evangelicals adhere to the authority of the Bible as God's inspired Word and, in Luther's terms, "the cradle that brings us the Christ." We love the Bible and seek to honor it in every way, including elevating it over man-made traditions such as doctrines.

Truth Matters Most

Let me back up and suggest something even more daring and perhaps radical. I believe that the ultimate standard that should govern all human thinking and acting is truth itself. Sadly, however, many church people and leaders act as if truth is a relatively minor issue; for them what matters more than truth is tradition. This reminds me of the old gospel song by evangelist Gypsy Smith, "If I Am Dreaming, Let Me Dream On." He wrote the song after being told by a skeptic that if he believed in the truth of the gospel he was dreaming. Too many evangelical Christians have treated the Christian life this way: "If I am dreaming, let me dream on." This appears in the ways in which evangelical leaders enforce orthodoxy; whether it is true or not is not as important as whether people under them adhere to it strictly and without reservation or qualification.

Now, I know that many conservative evangelicals reading this are thinking, "How dare he—an evangelical theologian—reduce doctrine to such a low level of importance!" That isn't what I intend. I teach and promote right doctrine but only insofar as it is biblical. I encourage my students to think about doctrines for themselves and to test every doctrine by its consistency with Scripture, and insofar as it is not clearly drawn from and supported by Scripture to question or even discard or relegate it to the category of *adiaphora* ("things indifferent").

The irony is that some of the conservative evangelicals who will raise objections to this chapter (and perhaps this entire book) have themselves dared at one time or another to question a doctrinal formulation. But too often once they are ensconced in a seat of authority, they tend to suffer from "hardening of the categories," by which I mean a rigidity and narrowness that disallows what they once practiced—honest, open, and scripturally faithful questioning of traditional beliefs and practices. I know people like that.

My proposal, then, is that every evangelical and everyone else recognize truth as the ultimate standard for belief and resist the temptation to "dream on" or pretend that something is unequivocally right and true just because it is traditional. Truth stands above everything but God, and God is the source and standard of all truth. Every human heart and mind, including the evangelical Christian's, should be on a constant quest for truth, which necessarily involves being open to the possibility that something once taught might turn out to be less than true and stand in need of revision. "Dreaming on" is to live in illusion rather than reality; surely God wants us to live in the real world and find out the truth about him regardless of what orthodoxies we may have to overturn in that quest.

Nineteenth-century English writer Samuel Taylor Coleridge once remarked that "he that begins by loving Christianity better than truth will proceed to love his own sect or church better than Christianity and end by loving himself better than all" (*Aids to Reflection*, Aphorism 25). There is great risk in denying the importance of truth even over doctrine. Generally speaking, even the most conservative evangelical who insists on the truth of orthodoxy will acknowledge this, but the proof is in the pudding. Most conservative evangelicals *act as if* what they really value is some man-made system of doctrine, such as nineteenth-century Reformed theologian Charles Hodge's three-volume *Systematic Theology* (which was first published in 1872 and has served as a standard of evangelical orthodoxy for over a hundred years) or some confessional statement such as the *Baptist Faith and Message*.

Some Baptist seminaries hold a ceremony at the beginning of each school year during which faculty have to go forward and sign some version (either 1925, 1963, or 2000) of the *Baptist Faith and Message*. What if a godly and learned faculty member said, "In good conscience I cannot sign it this year because over the summer I've studied the Bible with fresh eyes and I'm confident something in this man-made statement of faith is faulty"? What would happen to him or her? The real test is whether such a person's reasons would be heard and considered or whether he or she would be unceremoniously fired. That's the test of whether orthodoxy or the Bible matters most. I have known of cases where such situations were handled very differently.

I am not opposed to having written statements of faith even though I tend to be wary of them. They have a tendency to grow like a weed patch and accumulate all kinds of subarticles and modifiers and extensions. I once taught with a professor of theology who was under fire from some of the college's constituents because they claimed his ideas violated the statement of faith. However, they had trouble demonstrating it because the statement of faith did not explicitly rule out his controversial views. So, some of them argued that it extrudes a penumbra—like an aura—that is more than what is explicitly stated there; it is what is implied there. The natural question was, of course, "Implied to whom?" Written creeds and statements of faith have a way of giving rise to inquisitions, and they often become authorities functionally equal with Scripture—even among Baptists and other free church Protestants who claim to be "non-creedal"! This tendency should be resisted by evangelicals, but that requires the courage to challenge and press for change.

One evangelical college president suggested that professors who have mental reservations about the college's statement of faith leave and find somewhere else to teach. The problem is that not many years ago, during his own presidency, someone pointed out that the college's statement of faith contained a doctrinal error that no one had noticed before. The president agreed and the wording of that article was changed. Did he ask the person who pointed out the error to leave the college? I doubt it. But what would happen to a professor who challenged the wording of some article with which the president agreed? That might be a different matter.

Tradition without Traditionalism

My argument here is that every evangelical institution, including churches and denominations, should constantly reexamine their orthodoxies in the light of God's Word. That's the way to be truly evangelical. Such people might come out essentially to the same place where the creeds and traditions are, but at least they have come to it after a fresh look at Scripture and not simply "because the traditions say so." To be evangelical includes being reformed and always reforming. Conservatism among evangelicals manifests in a traditionalism that resists such critical reexamination even in the light of God's Word.

Suppose someone wants to counter this conservatism within his or her evangelical organization. What should such an enlightened leader do? I suggest every organization—religious or otherwise —that is concerned with truth appoint one person to be the paid asker of truth questions. Such a person would be like the court jester of medieval kings and queens, who could mock and ridicule the royal court without fear of punishment. He or she would be rewarded rather than punished for holding the organization accountable to truth. His or her constant question would be "But is this true?" His or her role would be to make impossible the inevitable tendency to hold tradition higher than truth. This seems to be such a pervasive problem even in evangelical organizations that I can consider only this strategy truly helpful in counteracting it. Who would want the job? Many would like to have it, but only those who have demonstrated a real commitment to truth and reality at any cost should be offered it. And it should come with tenure!

Being evangelical includes being committed to the authority of God's Word. Why? Because we believe it is true. Why? Because it brings us the Christ who has saved us and lives in our lives. How do we know? Because an entire population across centuries has witnessed to its life-transforming power. Like the U.S. Constitution the Bible serves as the evangelical "highest court of appeal" in matters of belief and practice; everything we believe and do should be justified by the Bible or at least by biblical principles. Anyone who disagrees with this is no longer an evangelical because this is the evangelical critical principle. Apart from it evangelical faith does not exist.

Yet the irony is that many conservative evangelicals act as if they do not really believe it. When a new idea pops up, they react immediately to counter it solely because it is new and not what has always been believed. No matter how much it is based on faithful biblical scholarship and interpretation, if it is not traditional most conservatives oppose it. One way to identify a conservative evangelical is by how often he or she jumps to resist or even declare as heresy new ideas compared with how often he or she proposes a new angle or aspect of the truth already known and believed. Surely all truth has not been captured already!

After proposing that evangelicals subject all orthodoxies, however ancient and accepted, to fresh and faithful reexamination in light of God's Word, I want to add that orthodoxy and tradition are not bad in and of themselves. Some evangelicals, especially in the pews but sometimes in the pulpits and lecterns, act as if only some "new truth" is valid and as if everything old is odious. This appears to be a weakness among at least some younger evangelicals in the emerging church movement; they need to recognize and acknowledge the value of tradition even as they relativize its authority. It's good to question authority in the sense of interrogate it in the light of Scripture, but it is another thing to execute it on the basis of culture and preference for the new and unusual. Those who ignore history or expel tradition are doomed to repeat its mistakes and reinvent the wheel. We all inherit some tradition and there is no such thing as traditionless interpretation of Scripture or worship or ethics. Every project of inquiry and investigation into truth works from within some tradition of values and beliefs. It is impossible to step out of tradition and community into some ethereal place where we take a look from nowhere. The view from nowhere does not exist. Why not embrace tradition while critically reflecting on it from within? That's what I recommend to young evangelicals who may be tempted to throw the baby of Christian tradition out with the bathwater of dead orthodoxy. The trick is to keep believing while questioning what is believed. To question is good, but to question everything all the time is impossible. (Readers intrigued by this might wish to read my book *Questions to All Your Answers: The Journey from Folk Religion to Examined Faith* [Zondervan, 2007]).

So what is the best way to approach this paradox? I recommend that every evangelical read a good book of church history that includes as plain and straightforward an account of the development of Christian doctrines as possible. There is no such thing as the "unvarnished truth," but objectivity is a good ideal to strive for. Find as objective an account of historical theology—the great tradition of Christian belief and teaching—as possible and immerse yourself in it. Before questioning doctrines, make sure you understand them. People who express doubts about the doctrine of the Trinity look foolish if they have never studied it and don't know what it really is. For example, the orthodox doctrine of the Trinity is not that God is "one in three and three in one." That's a contradiction. The classical doctrine carved out by the early church fathers over nearly a century is that God is *one substance and three persons* or, to put it in a more contemporary expression—*one what and three whos*. It's perfectly alright to question that so long as one knows what it is.

Moreover, it is good to know what answers have already been given to the questions. It is likewise helpful to think about what idea of God might replace the doctrine of the Trinity if that were to be discarded. My experience is that Christians who really study it come to believe in the classical doctrine of the Trinity more firmly than before. It is so often questioned and denied based on misunderstandings of it.

Some readers might be thinking: "Well, that's all well and good, but I don't see why doctrine is necessary at all. Why not just have spirituality without doctrine?" That's been tried as well, and people who have tried it always end up believing something and expecting others to believe it with them. It seems impossible to worship or experience God in a doctrineless vacuum! Worship and experience give rise to belief and belief serves worship and experience by giving them content and shape. A vague, noncognitive Christianity is always bland and ineffective. Dead or dogmatic orthodoxy is one danger, but a greater one is a spirituality consistent with everything. It's literally nothing.

I have urged especially younger evangelicals to hold onto the label "evangelical" and not discard it simply because some have wrongly identified it with rigid, narrow, and hardened orthodoxy. Evangelical faith is about experiencing God through Jesus Christ in accordance with the Bible. It is about being transformed by the Spirit of God more than being informed by doctrines. But that does not mean orthodoxy is a bad thing; it just needs constant reexamination and correction. It needs to be "reformed and always reforming" in the light of God's Word.

CHAPTER 2

BUILDING CHARACTER WITHOUT MORALISM

When I was studying for my doctorate at a major American university, several influential evangelicals founded a national organization to promote "Christian morality" in America. A student wrote an editorial for the university's student-run newspaper arguing that these Christians should be censored. He felt that they were "legislating morality" and portrayed the organization in question—and evangelical Christians in general—as judgmental. Unfortunately many Americans consider evangelical Christians judgmental, intolerant, and moralistic in a bad sense, even though every right-thinking person does acknowledge the necessity of a personal framework of morals.

Morality may have a bad reputation for several reasons, including the hypocrisy of so many moralists who tell people to live one way and live a different way themselves. Nevertheless, neither the individual nor society can get along without morals. At the simplest level they are nothing more or less than beliefs about right and wrong; everyone has them even if they deny it. If you doubt me on this, try stealing the car owned by a person who rejects morals. That person would suddenly discover and display his or her beliefs about right and wrong.

Of course, things are never as simple as this. People who openly acknowledge the necessity of morality argue endlessly about whether morals are absolute or relative, objective or subjective, cultural or universal. But those aren't the substance of our subject in this chapter; we'll leave those debates to philosophers. Instead, we turn to a different, if somewhat related, question: Do you have to be *moralistic* to be evangelical? Most people would say yes; being evangelical and being moralistic are inseparably connected. Having one without the other is unthinkable to many evangelicals. But is it really so? Much depends on what is meant by the terms *moralistic* and *moralism*.

Increasingly people use the label "moralistic" to describe persons and organizations who adhere to a rigid, black-and-white mentality about right and wrong and who refuse to recognize gray areas of behavior and decision-making. A moralistic person, in other words, is someone who constantly judges people's behaviors according to a presupposed, absolute set of ethical rules. Moralism, then, is the habit of the heart and mind that elevates right behavior, judged by a set of absolute standards, to extreme importance and determines the extent to which people are acceptable to God or society by their conformity to that.

Ask any number of people walking the malls of America whether evangelical Christians are moralistic and you will find them affirming it. Their picture of an evangelical is someone who is morally conservative and judgmental. The standards of behavior they use are perceived to be old fashioned, if not totally out of touch with modern or postmodern life. They are viewed as resistant to change or leniency; exceptions to rules are considered evidence of "situation ethics" — the view that moral rules are flexible depending on context — which evangelicals supposedly eschew.

This picture of evangelicals as conservative moralists to speak for God on matters of human behavior is probably exaggerated, but like all stereotypes there's some truth in it. My own life in the thick of American evangelical Christianity confirms the partial validity of it. And I'm afraid I've been guilty at times. Like many conservative evangelicals I have occasionally, or often (I hate to admit it), judged people's worth by their behavior. And

I've decided the rightness or wrongness of their behavior by my religious community's rules and norms. And my evangelical community's rules and norms have often been drawn more from tradition than from Scripture.

Let me offer some examples. When I was growing up in an evangelical church and in Youth for Christ, we were forbidden to dance or go to movies. Smoking tobacco and drinking alcohol were considered sure evidence of apostasy—falling away from grace onto a path straight for hell. And yet, many of my spiritual mentors loved to quote Charles Spurgeon and C. S. Lewis—two British evangelicals who were undeniably paragons of orthodoxy and virtue but who also smoked and drank alcohol. (Well, at least Lewis did both; I'm only sure that Spurgeon smoked!) Double standards and inconsistencies abounded, and that eventually led me to reconsider the moralism of my youth. Yet, like many evangelicals, I cannot shake it off entirely. When my daughters were in high school and wanted to go to the prom dance, I had to let my wife deal with that; I just couldn't handle it, so I went into denial about it. Trying to dance at my older daughter's wedding struck horror and shame in my heart. Even though I no longer considered it sinful, I didn't want to do it and knew I was terrible at it. The shame-based system of morality one grows up with dies hard.

But isn't there a good sense of moralism? Is all moralism of that stripe—rigid, unrealistic, judgmental, and harsh? What about simply discerning the wrongness of certain behaviors, such as abortion and homosexual acts (to say nothing of crimes)? Evangelicals have made a name for themselves by specializing in opposing these practices and condemning people who do them. They have been less famous for opposing injustice, racism, and poverty. Why? Because the grip of conservative morality drawn from decades of being obsessed with sexual sins has a strong hold on many evangelical Christians. There's an old joke that asks why Southern Baptists (but it could be almost any group of evangelicals) are against sex standing up. Why? The answer is because it might lead to dancing. If my mention of that joke shocks you,

you might be in the grip of conservative evangelical moralism that is often humorless and easily shocked by any mention of sex in public.

Shaking off Evangelical Moralism

My impression is that the public perception of evangelicals as generally too rigid in their morality and too moralistic toward outsiders (that is, sinful unbelievers) is all too true. While statistics show that practices such as sex before marriage and divorce are just about as common among evangelicals as any other group in society, evangelical spokesmen specialize in condemning them rather than dealing with them. There are exceptions, of course, but too many conservative evangelical ministers and other leaders are too focused on the dos and don'ts and casting stones at those who violate their codes of conduct.

One evidence of this is the way in which evangelicals handle their own leaders who fall into sin and are exposed as adulterers or thieves. Often those who fall are the very ones who were most vocal against the sins they were practicing. And the reaction to their fall is too often one of bewildered dismay, shock, and rejection. But why? Part of evangelical belief is that all are sinners; nobody is righteous except in God's eyes by grace through faith. Anyone who claimed to be sinless would be soundly criticized by most evangelicals. So why the shock and dismay when an evangelical leader turns out to be a sinner?

I'm not advocating winking at egregious sexual or financial misconduct. All I'm saying is that evangelicals could do better in such cases. We set ourselves up for trouble by being unrealistic about people's morality and pretending that anyone is above reproach. When a leader slips and falls into sin, we shouldn't be surprised; it should confirm our belief in total depravity! And then we should demonstrate our belief in grace by showering forgiveness and restoration on the repentant sinner. That doesn't mean we should revel in what theologian Dietrich Bonhoeffer called "cheap grace." But that's not a danger; if it were I'd be writing about that!

A far greater danger is judgmentalism toward outsiders and insiders and unrealistic expectations about human behavior.

Back to moralism. Here it denotes setting up a code of conduct that derives largely from tradition and seeks to enforce it on people with harsh sanctions for those who fall short of perfection. The Pharisees of Jesus' day were the moralists of their times. And Jesus, who held to strict moral standards of right and wrong, opposed them. Why were they moralists and Jesus was not? Because they lived by rules and sought to impose rules of conduct on others that were oppressive, unrealistic, and often without reasonable justification from Scripture. They were based on the "traditions of men" rather than the revealed will of God, and they left little to no room for grace and mercy.

Jesus did not specialize in rules; he specialized in principles such as love and mercy. His harshest words of criticism were reserved for those who rejected and condemned sinners without extending to them God's mercy and forgiveness. And he criticized those who focused too much on external behaviors to the neglect of inward dispositions and attitudes. For Jesus it was possible to keep the letter of the whole law of God and still be a rank sinner because of an unforgiving and hateful spirit. Similarly, it was possible to have a loving and kind spirit while falling short of perfect law-keeping and still be righteous.

Some people would probably consider Jesus a moralist because of his Sermon on the Mount (Matthew 5–7). But even a cursory glance at this passage shows just how nonmoralistic Jesus was. He specialized in relativizing rules of the religious elite and elevating sinners who repent to a higher status than the hateful keepers of the law. Does that mean Jesus didn't care about morals? Not at all. His standard of morality was higher and stronger than that of the religious moralists of his day; they specialized in inspecting the lives of lowly people to prove what great sinners they were and how righteous they — the Pharisees — were. Jesus set the bar of morality higher than the Pharisees did. He declared that motive is more important than outward action and called people to give themselves wholly to God's love rather than to rules of conduct.

Jesus didn't throw out all rules, of course, but he relativized them and put people higher than rules. The religious rules said that a person could not do any work on the Sabbath, but Jesus went around healing people on that day. When challenged, Jesus said the Sabbath was made for people, not people for the Sabbath. And he said that the heart's intentions and motives are more important in determining the rightness or wrongness of a behavior than conformity to rules.

Yes, some people would call Jesus a moralist. Christians on both the "right" and the "left" (that is, both conservative and liberal Christians) tend to view and portray Jesus as a champion of their moral causes. Jesus was either a leader of the Moral Majority of his day or else he was a first-century liberator of the oppressed. Neither portrait is correct; Jesus believed in and taught holiness of life without being a moralizing judge of everyone's behavior. And he certainly did not lead a campaign to impose his or anyone's morality on society. Jesus was a moralist only in the unusual sense that he spoke often and warmly of loving one's neighbor and showing mercy to people in need of forgiveness. You see, Jesus was more concerned about character than about morality insofar as morality means living according to an external code of behavior. Character is about being inwardly good; morality is about conformity to a moral standard. Character requires transformation of the heart; morality requires only fear of punishment.

Judging Like Jesus and Paul

Notice also that Jesus did not go around judging the behaviors of people outside the people of God; like the Old Testament prophets he was mainly concerned about the character of God's people. How the Romans or the Greeks behaved was apparently none of Jesus' concern. A true moralist will make universal judgments about people's lives and conduct and not focus on a particular group.

Jesus was not a true moralist in that sense. His concern was with Israel and those non-Hebrews who crossed his path and needed his help. He didn't embark on a crusade to make people morally righteous by law or even threat of divine punishment, and that's especially true of people outside those to whom God sent him — the descendants of Abraham through Isaac and Jacob. They were the people of God of Jesus' day (which is not to say nobody else could be saved). God's main concern with them, apparently, was repentance and amendment of character. He didn't send a new set of rules; almost no scholar thinks of the Sermon on the Mount as a new set of rules. Rather, he sent them a portrait of good character — Jesus and his teachings — and asked them to repent and allow God to change their hearts.

What about the rest of the New Testament? Was Paul or any other apostle a moralist? Not in the sense of that word used here. Certainly Paul and other apostles taught morality to Christians, but their focus was more on the transformation of heart (character) that resulted in good living than on rules of conduct or judging people's behavior. To the extent they did judge people's character and impose rules, it was aimed at God's people — the church — and not at society at large. To be sure, the apostles, like Jesus, were concerned with behavior and conduct but only among God's people.

Here is one place where conservative evangelicals have too often turned the New Testament on its head. We have specialized in moralism toward society outside the church while neglecting church discipline. The thrust of the New Testament is the other way around. Jesus and the apostles brought a message of character to God's people without suggesting that other people had to live the same way. They simply expected that those who were not God's people would always fall short of God's morality until and unless they repented and received the grace and mercy and transforming power of God into their lives through Jesus Christ and the Holy Spirit.

When Paul went to the Greeks in Athens and spoke to them about their belief in the "unknown god" (Acts 17), did he attempt to impose any moral rules or code of conduct on them? He did not. There and elsewhere he spoke of Jesus Christ and his resurrection and asked people to believe on him. Then, when people did repent and believe and entered into the fellowship of the church, Paul called them to allow God to transform their hearts and minds so that they would have the gift of good character. Out of that would flow true morality.

Conservative evangelicals today have largely missed the boat when it comes to morality. Too often they have focused on rules and on the behaviors of people outside the church. Too often they have either neglected church discipline or turned it into a method of rejecting people without realistic hope of restoration. If evangelicals really want to follow the New Testament pattern of ethics and morality, they would focus on character, the transforming work of God within people's hearts, and the morality of the church — especially its love for all who fall short of God's standards. The church's morality would then be about the natural change that occurs when people receive Jesus Christ and the Holy Spirit into their lives. And it would be about faith, hope, and love rather than external standards of conduct.

How to Promote Morality without Moralism

I don't want you to misunderstand me. I know from painful experience how easily that happens. I don't think evangelicals should ignore bad behavior. What I'm saying is that especially conservative evangelicals have too often practiced moralism rather than New Testament morality. Evangelicals don't have to do that; they can still be evangelicals while practicing and promoting New Testament morality. Here's how.

First, at their best evangelicals are not guardians of rules or judges of behavior; at their best evangelicals are promoters of an experience that results in transformed character. In other words, our approach to ethics should focus on God's power to change people's lives. We fail to be authentically evangelical insofar as we rely on an outward code of conduct and threats of punishment to reform people's lives. Our message is rather the good news that people can't reform their lives apart from an inward change called conversion.

That's precisely where many conservative evangelicals go wrong; they fall into the trap of believing that preaching morality can result in people changing. Perhaps some people will be affected by it, but more likely they'll simply hide their sins and pretend they don't exist. And the wrong attitudes and dispositions that give rise to them will continue unabated.

At their best evangelicals know that only the Holy Spirit can produce transformed character that results in genuinely ethical living. Rule keeping never makes people genuinely moral because real morality arises from within and is based on love for what is good and right. When I look back on my own youth in evangelicalism, I realize that what kept me from having premarital sex was not lack of opportunity or rules or fear of God. As a teenager I was "on fire" for Jesus; I considered myself (and other people considered me) a "Jesus freak." No, I wasn't particularly weird. I wasn't a hippie or anything like that; I was simply "turned on to Jesus." I didn't get involved in sex, drugs, alcohol, or smoking or anything else evil because God was doing his work in my life and I felt it and knew it and loved God and the things of God. I loved to attend church and worship God. I wasn't born that way, however; it came from powerful experiences of God that changed my life and produced in me the character that made me want to behave in a loving way toward God and other people.

None of this happened to me in isolation; the change was filtered to me through Christian communities: Youth for Christ, my home church (and especially my youth group at church), and my Christian friends. All of these communicated to me the nature of the transformed character God wants to create in a person; the focus was not on rules but on love—not the sentimental kind of love that results in occasional acts of kindness ("charity") but the genuine desire for other people's good—and the desire to make God delighted by my living.

There were rules, to be sure, but keeping them was treated as the result of the change of heart Christ wants to work in a person's life. No sex before or outside of marriage was not a burdensome rule that I had to keep; it was a way of pleasing God and treating myself and others with loving respect. As a result of my conversion and Spirit baptism it pleased me to honor God in that way. Did I still feel the pull of such sins? Of course. But resisting temptation and living a clean life was my inward desire and goal; it wasn't a task imposed on me or carried out because of fear. My clean living wasn't something I had to do; it was something I got to do. That's how I looked at it as a teenager.

That's authentic evangelicalism. It focuses attention on the transforming experience that introduces a person to friendship with Jesus Christ and delivers the inner desire and power to please him. It creates communities of character centered on the experience of becoming new creatures in Christ Jesus. Being a "new creature"—being "born again"—is the heart of evangelical faith. Unfortunately, too many evangelicals make their faith revolve around rules and judgment and shame.

Second, at their best evangelicals are not judges of people's behavior but cheerleaders of good character and conduct. Evangelicals know what God wants and therefore what good character looks like. The Bible couldn't be clearer: "You shall love the Lord your God with all your heart, and with all your soul, and with all your mind ... you shall love your neighbor as yourself." Or as St. Augustine put it: "Love and do as you please." Conservative evangelicals get nervous and think that the message of love isn't sufficient; people will take advantage of it and excuse all kinds of evil behavior so long as they satisfy themselves that they are loving God and their neighbor. True enough. That happens. But the best antidote to the poison of depravity is not laying down the law but instilling right desires, and only God can do that.

Our message to the world outside the borders of the church, then, should not be, "Behave yourselves and maybe God will accept you." Nor should it be, "You are all terrible sinners and we aren't, so let us show you the right way to live and perhaps even criminalize your wrong behavior so you don't corrupt us." That's the message many people outside evangelicalism hear, whether evangelicals put it that way or not.

Nowhere does the New Testament encourage Christians to judge the behavior of unbelievers. In fact, the apostle Paul tells the Corinthian Christians he and they are not to judge those outside the church but only those inside the church: "For what have I to do with judging outsiders? Is it not those inside the church whom you are to judge? God judges those outside" (1 Corinthians 5:12 – 13). In other words, when it comes to the bad behavior of non-Christians, leave it to God. Our task and joy as evangelicals is to hold out to outsiders the gospel of forgiveness and power to change. Their conduct is none of our business; our business is our own conduct, beginning with our hearts (desires).

Unfortunately, too many conservative evangelicals associated with the Religious Right have meddled in non-Christians' conduct and behavior in God's name. And they have attempted to legislate Christian morality, which is impossible. Christian morality is about receiving from God the gift of a character that loves to love and for which obeying God comes naturally and joyfully. It isn't about posting commandments on school or courthouse walls.

On Not Legislating Morality

So what about issues like abortion and homosexuality — two "hot topics" of ethics and morality especially associated with evangelicals because they have been in the forefront of opposing them. All evangelicals are likely always to oppose abortion-on-demand (i.e., abortion for convenience) because of our strong love for all people and belief that fetuses are at least potential people created in God's image and likeness. And evangelicals will probably always believe that homosexual behavior is wrong because it deviates from God's plan that sex should take place within a complementary relationship of marriage between a male and a female. The Bible indicates strongly that man without woman is incomplete and that they are meant for each other. The underlying principle is community between those who are different. But too much conservative evangelical reaction to abortion and homosexuality has been moralistic rather than truly evangelical.

For one thing, at their best evangelicals love the woman who seeks an abortion as much as the fetus about to be aborted. Rather than seeking to punish her or prevent her from having an abortion by law, we should do everything in our power and means to help women with unwanted pregnancies carry their unborn children to term and then either raise them or give them up for adoption. Too much of our energy has gone into criminalizing abortion and too little into preventing them or making them unnecessary. Also, too often conservative evangelicals have behaved as if they are the moral governors over society when Jesus has nowhere given us that mandate. We can decry injustice and evil in society without using our power to try to impose our own vision of truth, beauty, and goodness on people outside the church. But more important than decrying injustice and evil outside the church is our mandate simply to proclaim the good news of Jesus Christ and demonstrate the better way to live by being a light set on a hill.

So what about homosexuality? Conservative evangelicals have too often condemned homosexuals and their behavior or even sought to criminalize it. All evangelicals believe sex outside of marriage between a man and a woman is sinful, but we do not have to criminalize it or even go out of our way to focus attention on it as especially evil. Among ourselves, within our own communities of faith, we should proclaim God's power to change people's lives and help them live joyfully celibate lives if necessary. That's not only our message to homosexuals; it is also our message to people who do not find a marriage partner of the opposite sex. Chastity and celibacy are not evils or even terrible burdens. God can give a person the desire, will, and ability to live a chaste and even celibate life especially within a community soaked in the love of Christ and the power of the Holy Spirit. But we should come alongside such persons with friendship and support.

The proper evangelical attitude toward sinful behavior outside the church should be one of wise resignation and acceptance. There's no gospel call to change the world into the church by law. In fact, it cannot be done. Christian morality cannot be legislated because it has to do with the inward dispositions of the heart, not with outward and unwilling obedience to a set of rules. As evangelicals we can accept the fact that the world is under a different rule than we are; only when God's kingdom comes will God's will be "done on earth as in heaven." Until then, our focus should be on creating communities of virtue and character that sponsor and promote the Jesus lifestyle. These become our way of changing the world—by showing a better way to live.

Mennonite theologian John Howard Yoder wrote in *The Politics of Jesus* (Eerdmans, 1972, 1992) that Christians are not called to be managers of history or society. We are called to obey God and to be submissive to the rulers of the world insofar as their rules do not conflict with God's. I'm persuaded by his arguments from Scripture; nowhere do I see Jesus Christ or any apostle giving Christians a mandate to change the world by using political power. Our power is example and persuasion.

But, you may be asking, what about those extreme examples of horrendous injustices and violence in the world? Shouldn't we as Christians do our best to be "salt and light" by using whatever power we have to make the world a better place? Perhaps—but only as good citizens and not as Christians trying to impose our morality on everyone. Christians will probably disagree among themselves about some of these issues "out there." Some Christians believe capital punishment is evil; others believe it is right. Some would say it is a necessary evil. Can we come to agreement on this and then, as the body of Christ, attempt to legislate our consensus to either abolish it, keep it, or modify it? I doubt that will ever happen.

As a reasonable person who is also a citizen of this country and as a Christian, I have my opinion about capital punishment. When I vote, I think about this and other moral issues and why I want government to act in a certain way. Can I offer a good, rational, secular argument for my view? Or is my view wholly based on my Christian faith? If the former, I should probably campaign and vote for my opinion. If the latter, I should probably not expect non-Christians to agree with or obey my judgment about the matter. Fortunately, often it is not an either-or but a both-and. I can offer secular, rational reasons for my opinion about a moral issue *and* base it at least in part on my faith in Jesus Christ.

Being Salt and Light without Imposing Christian Morality

Some evangelical Christians will strongly disagree with my position here and consider it an abdication of Christian responsibility to Christianize secular society. Understand me, please. I'm not arguing that they are totally wrong, although I tend to lean in another direction. I happen to think Christianizing secular society is not a Christian calling. Being salt and light in the world is, but there are different ways of doing that. My preference is for the church to be salt and light by setting examples of communities of virtue and character centered on love.

But my main concern here is that people can be authentically evangelical and not be moralistic in the sense I've described in this chapter. That includes attempting to impose Christian morality on non-Christians. Those who think as I do have more biblical backing than others because the Bible is silent about any Christian campaign to make people who don't have any relationship with Jesus Christ be moral.

So what about those who do have a relationship with Jesus Christ? Should evangelicals promote good morality to them? Of course. Churches should foster strong Christian character by modeling virtues that give rise to good morals. And they should be places where people meet the living God in life-transforming encounters that instill within them desire to please God. There will be cases, of course, where rules have to be imposed and punishments for violating them exacted. Such rules should only be enforced, however, when someone claiming to be a Jesus person is living an unrepentant life that is clearly contrary to the Jesus life.

Each church will no doubt have somewhat different versions of these rules. And punishments should always be focused on restoration and not revenge or exclusion. A clear example is given by Paul in 1 Corinthians 5, where he commands the Corinthian church to excommunicate the member who is living in sin with his stepmother. Later, in 2 Corinthians, he urges them to receive him back into fellowship because he has repented. This is not moralism but healthy discipline or tough love.

Conservatives tend to fall into moralistic attitudes and behaviors; evangelicals do not have to be conservative in that sense. Conservative moralism is about making people behave using rules and shame; evangelical morality is about fostering an environment where God's Spirit can inculcate the desire to please God through a life of obedience. Moralism is outward and focused on judgments; evangelical morality is inward and focuses on transformation of persons.

CHAPTER 3

CELEBRATING AMERICA
WITHOUT NATIONALISM

My wife and I visited friends in another state on the Sunday closest to July 4. He served on the staff of the state's largest church — a conservative evangelical church noted for its marvelous holiday productions. This was its "God and Country" celebration. A full orchestral band played the "hymns" of the various branches of the military and color guards marched down the aisles with the branches' flags and banners. The atmosphere was highly charged with fervent patriotism. People who served in the military were asked to stand and be honored when their branches' colors paraded through the sanctuary. A United States senator prayed for our country and its fighting men and women. The sermon was about God's special favor on America.

This scene is repeated in thousands of conservative evangelical churches every summer. Many Christians simply take it for granted that worship near July 4 will look and feel something like this — even if not quite as elaborate. I grew up singing patriotic hymns in worship around Memorial Day, Independence Day, and Veterans Day. Few people think to question this custom of American conservative evangelicals, but for some years now — especially since living for a year in Germany — I've become uncomfortable with it.

Patriotism without Nationalism

In this chapter I want to talk about evangelical faith and nationalism. Especially since World War II evangelical Christians in America have tended to become increasingly nationalistic; most evangelical churches celebrate Independence Day (the Fourth of July) with special "God and Country" worship services. Sometimes these are elaborate stage presentations with military flags, bands, and fireworks displays. Almost always they include singing patriotic hymns such as the "The Star Spangled Banner," the "Battle Hymn of the Republic," and "America the Beautiful."

There is probably no more patriotic slice of the American population than evangelical Christians. I grew up in the thick of that. To this day I can't hear the national anthem or recite the pledge of allegiance to our flag without getting all choked up. It's programmed into me. So, I do consider myself patriotic. I love America and I pray that God will bless her and "mend her every flaw." There's a difference, however, between being patriotic and being nationalistic. It's a fine line hard to find and yet it is there, and evangelicals need to pay attention to it. Nationalism is a form of idolatry; it is idolatry of nation, people, blood, soil, and too often race. It's not unique to America; it has been the source of many wars and even genocides down through the centuries but especially in the nineteenth and twentieth centuries.

Nationalism is expressed in the old cliché "my country right or wrong," or even more in the saying "America — love it or leave it." While there is some truth in these mottos, they are too often exclaimed with heat; they are jabs aimed at people who dare to question the American government's policies and especially its war policies and practices. Too many people fail to observe the difference between love of country and slavish agreement with or obedience to the state and government. Nationalism often appears as conservative traditionalism and resistance to any sweeping or radical changes in society. And it rears its ugliest head in hatred aimed at noncitizens beyond the nation's borders or within them. But, at its best, nationalism is simply worship of country even if "country" signifies an ideal such as "the American way."

Most people who engage in nationalistic rituals and make nationalistic claims are not aware that they are practicing idolatry, but then who thinks they are idolaters? Nobody. So simply to say, "People don't mean to worship country," doesn't resolve the idolatry question; no one thinks they worship anything but the "true God." Idolatry, however, appears whenever people invest absolute, ultimate worth in and give uncritical loyalty to something other than God.

Patriotism is different from nationalism although the two may look alike at times. Patriotism is simply love of country and strong desire to see it flourish and prosper; it is displayed in loyalty to country and participation in the rituals and ceremonies that fly the nation's banner. A patriot is someone who is willing to die or suffer for the sake of country; he or she prays for the country and works hard to make it better and stronger.

Have I just melted the difference between nationalism and patriotism? Not at all. Look at what patriotism is not: uncritical loyalty and obedience to the state or government, belief that the country is better than any other and especially chosen or favored by God, and worship of country alongside or above God by expressing its ultimate worth. A nationalist is also a patriot, but a patriot is not necessarily a nationalist. A patriot loves country but doesn't necessarily worship it and feels loyal to it without necessarily thinking it is perfect or above the rest of humanity. Is nationalism simply patriotism "on steroids"? I don't think so. I consider nationalism different in kind and not only in degree from patriotism even though a single person can be both.

I consider myself a patriot. I would gladly die for my country if it were under attack and dying is the only way to protect and preserve it. That's because I think America is great; it is the "land of the free." But I'm not a nationalist because I think there are other lands of the free and I believe America is only a qualified good. It is not God or side-by-side with God or even especially favored by God above all other countries.

Evangelical American Nationalism

This is where nationalism especially appears among conservative evangelicals: in the belief that America is especially chosen and raised up by God to be a "Christian nation" bringing the whole world to God and the American way. My thesis here, however, is that one can be more evangelical by not being nationalistic in spite of the empirical fact that many evangelicals—especially the conservative kind—are nationalists. It's okay for evangelicals to be patriotic, but I will argue nationalism and authentic evangelical faith contradict each other even though they are often held together within the same breast.

Whether American nationalism is endemic to conservatism in America and among evangelicals is difficult to prove, but I take for granted that it is apparent. Conservatives, whether evangelical or not, tend to be flag-waving, uncritical loyalists to the American nation. Especially conservative evangelicals engage in revisionist history to try to prove that America was founded as a Christian nation; for them much is at stake in this project. They would like to turn America "back to God," which often means back to the golden age when America was thoroughly Christian. And they want to export the American way (free market capitalism, individualism, and democracy) to other countries along with the gospel; the two are often so confused in conservative mission efforts that it is nearly impossible to separate them.

Rarely is this done consciously; many conservative evangelical missionaries and evangelists claim they leave their cultural baggage at home when they fly to a foreign mission field. However, too often they subtly indoctrinate their converts not only into the gospel but also into Americanism. I know this to be true because I have taught the sons and daughters of evangelical missionaries for twenty-five years and they and some of their parents' converts come into my office and share their qualms with me. They've taken a class in anthropology or sociology and discovered that much that their parents or missionary mentors promote is really American lifestyle rather than gospel.

I should provide a few examples of conservative evangelical nationalism as I mean it. A colleague of mine who happened to be a Canadian citizen wanted to teach in his local evangelical church's vacation Bible school. The leaders of the VBS led the children and teachers in the pledge of allegiance to the United States and Christian flags at the beginning of each day. As a Canadian citizen my colleague declined to participate and the VBS officials asked him not to teach because of that. They put a national symbol above Christian fellowship and sound biblical teaching. (My colleague was an educated professor at an evangelical college.) That's as much as to elevate it to the status of an idol.

In another example, a friend of mine pastors a large church in an urban setting. He preached a series of sermons on the myth of a Christian nation and called his congregation to be critical of the American government insofar as it strays from standards of just war. A thousand people left his church in the subsequent weeks. They could not stand to hear America criticized. Of course, my friend wasn't criticizing America; he was criticizing Christians who blindly accept and support whatever the current American administration decides to do. But he also declared with good biblical support and support from the church fathers that no City of Man (nation) is the City of God (kingdom of God) and therefore a believer should never invest ultimate or absolute worth or loyalty to a country.

These two illustrations drawn from real life may help shed some light on a certain pervasive, conservative mentality that is all too common among evangelicals but is totally unnecessary for being evangelical. There's nothing about being evangelical that requires nationalism of that sort or really any sort. In fact, evangelical faith doesn't even require patriotism even though I think patriotism is a good thing. But I won't quarrel with someone who doesn't agree with me. I've encountered God-fearing, Bible-believing, Jesus-loving Christians who don't have a patriotic bone in their bodies. Some of them are in the Anabaptist churches, also known as "peace churches."

The fact that nationalism is not necessary for evangelical faith really sunk in to me when my family and I lived in Germany for a year. We got to know Christians of several denominational backgrounds and discovered that in Germany, since World War II, Christians are wary of nationalism. They know from their own history how destructive that mixture of religion and national pride can be. During the Nazi era of the 1930s and 1940s Hitler's party and government used that mixture to take over, dominate, and silence dissent among Christians. There and then, as among some evangelicals in America today, anyone who dared to criticize the regime was considered anti-German even if they stood on solid biblical grounds to do it.

Today it is difficult to find German flags (which are not the swastika flags of the Nazis, of course) flying or hanging in German churches. Because of that history they shy away from any kind of national celebration or symbolism in the church worship spaces. And they welcome Christians from all countries into their churches on an equal footing.

Of course, even the most conservative evangelical Americans think they do the same thing; they believe people of all nationalities are equally welcome and treated equally in their churches. But put yourself in the shoes of a citizen of another country who comes to an evangelical (or any) church on "God and Country" Sunday. What will they think and feel? What would you think and feel if you attended an evangelical church in another country and experienced a worship service that centered around national pride? I would wonder what was going on there. I would feel excluded. But the gospel is supposed to transcend nationality, and so should worship and Christian fellowship.

American Civil Religion

That last claim might provoke some dispute among conservatives. Isn't America God's favorite country in the world? Aren't we chosen by God in some special way that is not true of any other country? This is a deeply ingrained sentiment among conservative evangelicals and others. Many who never darken the door of a church believe it. I call it a form of American folk religion. Sociologists call it civil religion—a kind of implicit spirituality centered on country.

But is that biblical? That should be the key evangelical question—not whether it is popular or traditional. Like many evangelicals in America, I grew up thinking America is especially favored by God and called by God to save the world through missions and the export of the "the American way." That "American way" was, to my mind and the minds of my elders, capitalism and democracy. But the package also tended to include individualism and consumerism. We didn't think that, but it was true nevertheless. We confused together Christianity, democracy, capitalism, individualism, and consumerism. To our way of thinking exporting churches and malls automatically go together!

Even if you don't think in those fairly extreme terms about America and Christianity, you might be inclined to think that America was raised up and given a special destiny by God to be a light to the nations. Often the crucial term linked to this belief is "freedom." America supposedly has freedoms lacking in other countries. We have freedom of religion and freedom of speech. And we do, up to a point. But so do other countries. My family and I were shocked at the extent to which the freedoms we thought were unique to America abounded in Germany and other European countries.

Nevertheless, I will grant that America has been a great beacon of freedom lighting history since 1776. And I love that part of my national heritage. Yet I don't see anything especially evangelical about that. I can tout my nation's great ideals and influence without connecting that with God or evangelical Christian faith. As an evangelical Christian I feel at one with evangelical Christians around the world of any nationality, and I am loathe in any way to suggest that my country is somehow more closely connected with being Christian than theirs. I believe a person can be evangelical and love his or her own country and not think America is anything special. I happen to think America *is* special (I'm patriotic!), but that has nothing to do with being evangelical.

Many conservative evangelicals (and nonevangelical conservatives) try to demonstrate that America was uniquely founded on Christian principles. They point to the prayers and pious statements of George Washington, Thomas Jefferson, James Madison, John Adams, and Patrick Henry. There's no doubt that these men and many others among America's founding fathers spoke often and warmly about God. But were they Christians? Yes, they were members of Christian churches. And yet evangelicals are the first to say that merely being a member of a Christian church does not make a person authentically Christian (any more than being in a garage makes one a car!). Spouting pious platitudes does not make a person a real Christian; evangelicals know that well. So why do conservative Christians so often claim these founding fathers as some of their own? Were they, indeed, evangelical Christians or nominal Christians? And did they intend to base the new American republic on the Bible and Christianity, as many conservatives claim?

The record is mixed; both sides—those who claim these founding fathers were Christians and founded America on Christian principles and those who deny that—can point to much evidence. My own study of the matter leads me to believe most of the founding fathers were far from being evangelical Christians; they were more influenced by deism even though they were members of mainline Christian denominations, such as the Episcopal Church. A scholarly (yet readable) study of the matter is Frank Lambert's *The Founding Fathers and the Place of Religion in America* (Princeton University Press, 2003). Lambert, who has no axe to grind, demonstrates conclusively from the writings and speeches of the founding fathers that some of them leaned more closely to classical Christianity than others, but overall and in general they were not traditional, orthodox Christians.

That says nothing about their salvation, of course; neither Lambert nor I am interested in that which is solely God's business. The question is whether those conservative historians are correct who claim that all or most of the founding fathers were evangelical or orthodox Christians. The record is clear; they were not.

But that does not settle the question of whether America was founded on Christian principles. The founding fathers may or may not have been orthodox, believing Christians. (None of them, with the possible exception of Patrick Henry, was recognizably evangelical!) Were they Christian enough to base their new American republic on Christian or even Judeo-Christian concepts? The answer is not clear; it's ambiguous at best. Some of the founding fathers, for example, believed it is impossible to have objective morality—absolutes of right and wrong—without God as the moral governor of the universe. But most deists believed that as well. (Deists did not believe Jesus Christ is God incarnate or that God is triune.) The Enlightenment philosopher Immanuel Kant and even the Enlightenment skeptic Voltaire believed that! That's hardly a Christian idea.

Specifically regarding our founding fathers, Thomas Jefferson expressed serious doubts about crucial Christian beliefs such as the deity of Jesus Christ. George Washington may have been relatively orthodox in his Christian beliefs, but his main commitments seemed to be to the secret fraternal organization Freemasonry. James Madison was an orthodox Christian who wanted Christian principles such as belief in the depravity of man embedded in the structure of the republic. Compromise was the outcome; the structure of the republic's new government with "checks and balances" was based on the belief that power corrupts, which can come either from the Bible and traditional Christian doctrine or from revolutionary thinking.

So, there is no easy way to settle the question about the alleged Christian foundation of the American republic. There seem to be some Christian ingredients in it and some that are not particularly Christian. That's not to say any of the ingredients (concepts, ideals) are anti-Christian; few believe that! But many countries have come to incorporate ideas and principles compatible with Christianity in their constitutions. Many conservatives point to the words of the Declaration of Independence penned largely by

Thomas Jefferson that refer to nature and "nature's God." But that could be written by any deist, and "Providence" (a favorite word for God in the founding fathers' writings) was widely used by deists as a term for their god—a distant and impersonal moral governor of the universe. Note too that the United States Constitution nowhere mentions God.

The upshot of all this is that America may have been founded in part on Christian beliefs and principles. But the amalgam of the foundation was a mixture of many ingredients; at best orthodox Christianity was only one of them. All may be compatible with Christianity, but that would not be unique to America's founding. None of that settles the question whether America is a nation especially called and raised up by God. This idea originated with the Puritan settlers of New England and it spread throughout the colonies and became part of American culture's DNA. But what is its biblical basis? What historical evidence is there except America's large church member population and its power and world dominance? Does being the "world's only superpower" point to a special divine purpose and calling? Does having a population with many church members and attendees prove that America plays a special role in divine providence? I don't see that they do.

It seems to me that America's special divine calling, purpose, and empowerment is a popular folk myth. That is not to denigrate the amazing Christian missionary movements in America in the nineteenth century or the Great Awakenings and other revivals that have been such an integral part of its history. It is only to say that there is little basis for a claim that America is uniquely God's favored country. God uses many countries in history and there are many in the world today with large Christian populations that send missionaries to America!

Separation of Church and State

Another popular idea promoted by conservative evangelicals is that evangelical Christians (or just orthodox Christians) make better government officials. I know conservative evangelicals who would never dream of voting for any candidate for public office who was not evidently Christian. However, the great Protestant Reformer Martin Luther said he would rather have a competent Turk (Muslim) than an incompetent Christian as his prince. What did he mean? That being a Christian does not automatically make a person capable of governing and that the skills needed for good governing are not specific to any religion.

Conservative Christians who vote or campaign only for overtly Christian candidates seem to ignore two things. First, remember that America is a pluralistic society that guarantees the separation of church and state. Second, good government is seen as a matter of good values (not necessarily religious ones) combined with reason, vision, and organizational skills.

What about separation of church and state? Many conservative evangelical writers and speakers are claiming this is a bogus concept foisted on America to privatize Christian faith and squelch Christian voices in the public square. I would be the first to agree with them if that is what it meant. Some secularists misuse it that way, but the phrase itself was never meant to do that. Separation of church and state was originally coined by Thomas Jefferson in a letter to a Baptist association in New England who were concerned about having to pay church taxes to other denominations and about the fact that only members of certain denominations could serve in the state legislatures. Jefferson referred to a "wall of separation between church and state," by which he meant that no single denomination (or probably religion) should dominate American life and that no person should be marginalized or treated as less than equal because of his or her religious affiliation (including no religious affiliation).

Many conservative evangelicals have criticized separation of church and state because it has been misused by some liberals and secularists to argue that Christians should not attempt to influence government. For example, one civil liberties organization declared it a violation of separation of church and state when Catholic bishops warned Catholic members of Congress and legislators not to vote in favor of abortion rights. The Catholic bishops said that Catholic lawmakers who voted for abortion rights might be subject to excommunication from the Catholic Church. The secular civil liberties organization shouted "violation of separation of church and state!" as if something in the Constitution forbids churches from disciplining their own members.

That's simply ridiculous. Contrary to what some secularists and liberal Christians maintain, separation of church and state does not mean that churches and religious groups cannot attempt to persuade government toward their vision of right and wrong. What it does mean is that no church or denomination or religious organization can dominate government or hold a privileged position in or with government.

Some conservative Christians have overreacted to the liberal and secular misuses of the concept of separation of church and state so that they want to abolish it. They like the idea that Congress shall make no law prohibiting the free exercise of religion (Second Amendment to the Constitution), but the "wall of separation between church and state" they would like to tear down so that Christianity can claim and attempt to hold a special, privileged status as the conscience of government.

One conservative television pastor made a video documentary entitled "What if America Were a Christian Nation?" and spoke to the issue of a "theocracy." (Many critics of the Religious Right in America have said it would like to create a theocracy.) The minister defined "theocracy" as a church run by the government. In fact, however, theocracy means a government run by a church (or religious organization or person). Literally, it means a state governed by God. The conservative evangelical minister had it backwards; he wanted separation of church and state to protect church from government. That's all well and good; it does mean that. However, just as importantly it protects government from being dominated by any religion, denomination, or religious organization. It forbids theocracy, and many, if not most, evangelical Christians wanted that in the late eighteenth and early nineteenth centuries when many states still imposed a universal tax supporting a specific state denomination and required elected officials to belong to that denomination.

On the one hand, undoubtedly separation of church and state has been misused to silence especially conservative evangelical Christians in places like public schools. There have been egregious examples of teachers and principals attempting to hinder students and teachers from exercising their rights to free expression. For example, some public schools have intimidated teachers into staying away from the "Meet You at the Pole" rallies where mostly evangelical Christian students meet at the flagpole once annually before school begins to pray for the school and each other. There's no good reason why teachers shouldn't be able to be there and support this healthy expression of spiritual concern by students.

On the other hand, some conservative evangelicals have argued that since America is a "Christian nation" founded on Christian principles, prayer (and they mean Christian prayers) should be a part of every public school day. They don't seem to understand that such organized prayers written and led by principals and teachers would marginalize and intimidate students whose religious faith or lack of one falls into conflict with the prescribed prayers. For example, such prescribed public praying in Utah might be Mormon; how would evangelical Christian students feel there? Evangelicals should empathize with non-Christian students and not try to impose their own faith and practices on others. If they do, they give license to other religions or atheism to impose their faith or lack of it on students as well.

Many evangelicals are not in favor of organized, public praying in public schools—and that for very good reasons. Although public schools should teach community values such as compassion and honesty, they should not be centers of evangelism or indoctrination for any religious group. Students of all faiths or none at all should feel comfortable in public schools. In fact, I would argue that an evangelicalism that empathizes with non-Christian and nonreligious teachers and students is more authentically evangelical than one that tries to impose itself on them.

Forced evangelism is not true evangelism; enforced piety is no piety at all. The influence of Christianity in public schools should be from Christian kids who are equipped to live out the gospel among their peers at school and elsewhere.

Not a "Christian Nation"

I believe that many conservative evangelical Christians are missing the boat when it comes to issues of nation and state. Somehow they have adopted the false notion that America is a Christian nation rather than a melting pot or tossed salad (or whatever metaphor one prefers for pluralism) of many ethnicities and religious affiliations. Without doubt Christianity has been part of the great "glue" than has held the American experiment together and it is part of what makes America great. But America is not itself a Christian nation; its public square is like a village green in old New England where people of many different philosophies and faiths come together to negotiate their common life. Christians have as much a right to speak in that public square as anyone else, but they do not have a right to claim special privilege to dominate the conversation.

Conservative evangelicals also miss the boat when they elevate America to the status of a near idol by engaging in worship that blends God and country as if the two are inextricably linked together. As one of my colleagues who teaches worship says, good worship is never of "God and...." It is always of God alone. I believe that means American flags should be removed from Christian worship spaces so that nobody confuses the worship of God with veneration of nation. American flags can be present at Memorial Day and Independence Day church picnics, but worship should be focused on God alone and should not even hint at the idolatry of nationalism.

Some readers will wonder whether I love America. I do. I'm a patriot and I love to recite the pledge of allegiance and sing the national anthem. I love fireworks displays on the Fourth of July and parades that celebrate America's victories in just wars such as

World War II. But I do not associate all that with my evangelical faith; they are two different things. A person can be authentically and fully evangelical without being nationalistic because Jesus Christ and the gospel transcend nationality, and there is no hint in Scripture that any country since Old Testament Israel is especially favored by God.

CHAPTER 4

SEEKING TRUTH WITHOUT CERTAINTY

A newly converted college sophomore made an appointment to see me in my office. As he sat across my desk and began speaking, I knew he was in distress. His problem was a common one: he wanted to know how he could be absolutely certain about the truth of his new-found faith. What proof could I offer him that Christianity is true? I'm afraid I disappointed him; he went away disillusioned because neither I nor anyone else could take away the last shred of doubt from his mind.

One characteristic I have found almost universally true of self-proclaimed conservatives among America's evangelicals is a profound desire to achieve and maintain certainty in their beliefs about God and the Bible. I was one of them. As I was growing up I wanted nothing more than to be certain of all the answers to important questions related to our faith. When I couldn't figure out or understand the answers, I simply assured myself that someone—probably one of my older mentors such as a youth evangelist—understood them and was certain of their truth.

Becoming Comfortable with Doubt

You see, I was always an inquiring mind. My father was a pastor and at least pretended to be absolutely certain about everything he preached and taught. I can still see him standing in the pulpit holding his Bible and hear him saying to the congregation "If you doubt what I'm saying, search the Scriptures for yourselves and you'll find the answers there. Don't believe it because I say it; find it in the Bible." The upshot of his statements and the way he preached generally was that real Christians could have absolute certainty that all the teachings of our church were correct.

I realize, of course, that I'm interpreting all that through the lens of decades of later experience. Memory can be tricky; perhaps things weren't so black and white and certainty wasn't quite as resolute as my memory tells me. But for years after I grew up and left my father's church and denomination, I felt guilty because I didn't have that certainty my father and my spiritual mentors talked about. I questioned everything and felt bad about it. But the fact is that my father was largely responsible for my inquiring mind; behind the scenes at home he was pretty good at critical thinking and more than a few times I heard him express doubts about even some of the doctrines of our denomination. He even changed his mind about some pretty important matters over the course of his fifty-plus years of ministry. That shaped my thinking a lot; I grew up more than a little confused because I felt I needed certainty in order to be a mature and "solid Christian," yet I harbored nagging doubts about many of the "truths" I was supposed to accept without question.

My sojourn through a fundamentalist Bible college made things worse. The only reason I appeal to my own experience here (and elsewhere in this book) is because I really do believe it is not unique to me. Over the years I've met and conversed with numerous people whose experiences match my own. Almost every year of my twenty-five-year teaching career in three evangelical Christian universities I've dealt with students like me back then — feeling guilty and confused because they couldn't help having doubts and questioning doctrines and concepts they were told to believe without mental reservation.

Many of them attended colleges like mine. There I attempted to get answers to my questions, but I was soundly rebuffed merely for asking questions. I was just supposed to believe certain things with a level of assurance and confidence that excluded any nagging doubts or further seeking of answers. The Germans have a saying that fits the way I was taught theology in college: "Eat up, little birdies, or die."

Here I want to assure questioning and doubting evangelicals that it is okay to question and doubt so long as that questioning and doubting are honest and sincere and not chronic skepticism that refuses to settle down and live comfortably with ambiguity and uncertainty. In fact, honest questioning and doubting can give vitality to faith. Christian author Frederick Buechner writes: "Doubts are the ants in the pants of faith; they keep it awake and moving" (*Beyond Words: Daily Readings in the ABC's of Faith* [HarperOne, 2004]). Theologian Paul Tillich wrote that doubt is an essential aspect of faith; without doubt faith becomes false certainty like whistling in the dark and pretending nothing's wrong when you're afraid.

Conservative evangelicals and especially fundamentalists have long treated doubt as a sign of lack of faith and held up certainty as the signal of mature Christianity. Not all have abused inquiring and doubting minds as my college did, but too often they make the doubting Thomases among evangelicals feel ashamed merely for having honest and sincere questions about the Bible and traditional Christian doctrines. Even if they don't intend to do it, their emphasis on certainty leads to a totally unnecessary bad conscience among the intellectually alive and seeking people in their fellowships.

Many of those mostly young inquirers leave their evangelical spiritual homes and wander off into liberal churches. That just reinforces the conservatives' impression that doubting and questioning are a slippery slope down into liberal theology. In fact, the slippery slope away from evangelical faith for many people begins with the shame they feel for being intellectually curious and harboring honest and sincere doubts among their evangelical friends.

Conservative Theology, "Facts," and False Certainty

Conservative evangelicals specialize in dispelling doubts about doctrines and "facts" of the Bible and Christian belief. They produce seemingly erudite volumes (and DVDs) of apologetics aimed as much or more at questioning Christians as at skeptics. Don't get me wrong; I don't have anything against pointing inquiring minds to answers when the answers are available. My problem is that many of these conservative evangelical tomes of apologetics leave much to be desired when it comes to offering the certainty they claim to offer. I have come to believe that proof of the truth of important Christian doctrines is not available to us — at least not proof that leaves no room for doubt or questioning.

There are two reasons for this. First, we humans are finite and that condition will continue until we see God face to face. We live before the future *parousia* (unveiling) when all will be made clear. Even the apostle Paul admitted that now we (including he) see through a glass darkly and now we know only in part; we will only know the things of God perfectly when we see him face to face (1 Corinthians 13:12). That means certainty and complete understanding — lack of any possibility of doubt — is what theologians call eschatological. It's future; it belongs to the time when God shows himself to everyone and leaves no doubt about his being and his truth. That complete revelation is not yet. Now absolute certainty belongs to God alone and perhaps to a few who have received a rare and special gift to rise above all doubt for a time.

The second reason absolute proof of the truth of Christianity and its doctrines is lacking is our human condition of fallenness. Our minds are clouded by sin even if we have the Holy Spirit and the inspired Scriptures; we are not able to grasp truth with certainty beyond a shadow of doubt. That is not to say that doubt is a sign of sin; it is simply to say that alongside our finitude (by which I mean living before the completion) is our fallenness that adds to our inability to know perfectly, completely, or with absolute certainty. The human mind is capable of doubt and doubt it will. Those who claim to have no doubts are probably fooling themselves and maybe others.

It seems folksy to bring into this discussion a moment from a Southern gospel music video, but I will do so anyway. The reason is because it gave me tremendous comfort in my condition of more than occasionally having twinges of doubt about the truths to which I have committed my life. On one of the many Gaither Homecoming videos where gospel songwriter and singer Bill Gaither brought numerous old-time Southern gospel performers together to sing their songs of faith, one elderly singer expressed his struggle with doubt about heaven. He attributed those doubts to the devil, but he didn't suggest that his doubting was anything abnormal. Tears streamed down his cheeks as he confessed to it.

Then, one by one, other singers both old and young stood to tell about their own struggles with doubt. These were heroes of conservative Christianity who had written and sung the songs of faith for decades. One younger gospel quartet member told about his struggles with doubt after being diagnosed with cancer. He shared with the audience of gospel artists and the untold millions who would eventually view the video at home or on television that the first image coming to his mind when diagnosed was his last breath on his deathbed and fear of what came next—even though he was a committed evangelical who believed such doubts were ungodly.

That portion of that Gaither Homecoming video was the most real of all; rarely do conservative evangelical Christians open up and admit such doubts in the maturity of their faith. The one elderly singer's testimony opened a floodgate of reality as other, mostly younger men and women felt free to share their own struggles with doubt. Then the great Bill Gaither, author of hundreds of songs sung in most evangelical churches throughout the 1960s through the 1990s, sang a little-known piece he had written to express his own doubts and insecurities:

I believe, help Thou my unbelief. I walk into the unknown trusting all the while.

I long so much to feel the warmth that others seem to know, but should I never feel a thing, I'll trust him even so.

The crowd of a hundred or so notable evangelical recording artists sat there stunned — not because they now questioned Gaither's faith but because of the honesty and reality of the moment they had all just experienced. Oh, that more evangelicals could live in that reality where it is okay to say, "I'm not absolutely sure; I have my honest doubts and questions. God help me in my unbelief."

Not a Leap of Faith but Inward Assurance

In the New Testament a man came to Jesus asking him to heal his child. Jesus asked about his faith. The man said, "I believe; help my unbelief" (Mark 9:24). Jesus did not send him away and tell him to come back when his faith was complete without any mixture of doubt or uncertainty. He honored the man's little faith and his honesty and healed his son.

It's true that the New Testament makes a negative example of Jesus' disciple Thomas, who has acquired the moniker "doubting Thomas." But one has to wonder if the other disciples were any stronger in their faith; they had already seen the risen Lord, but what was their state of mind before that? Doubting Thomas seems to be an example of the human condition rather than an example of weak faith. What evangelical Christian, however mature in his or her faith, can say truly and honestly, "I never doubt or question any part of the content of Christian teaching. I live in total certainty of the truth all the time"? Yet that's the picture we who grow up in the evangelical movement often acquire from our elders: that genuine, mature Christian faith rises above all possibility of doubt and questioning and rests calmly and confidently in total assurance of the truth of what we believe.

This is one of the reasons I personally decline invitations to debate atheists. Such invitations come my way from time to time because I teach theology at a major Christian university and have a Ph.D. in religious studies from a secular university. Usually such inviters expect me to come sweeping into the debate, set the requirement of personal faith without doubt as the bar, and prove God to a skeptical audience. I've come to believe that's not realistic, not because my faith has become weaker but because it has become more real and honest. I believe in God, in Jesus Christ, and in the gospel, but I don't think I can prove any of that to someone who has never had any experience of God analogous to what I've had.

In fact, I don't think any of it is amenable to proof unless God himself chooses to reveal himself to a person in a way impossible to doubt or question. It seems that perhaps Moses and Paul were two like that in the Bible. And I've had some personal experiences of God encountering me and speaking to me and doing miracles in and through me that helped me settle confidently into my faith in him. But I still get up some mornings and wonder, "Was that just my imagination? Did that really happen? Was it really God?" That's not because I fell into sin while sleeping; it's just because I'm merely human. To try to convince someone else to have stronger belief based on proof than I have is unreasonable and dishonest.

None of that means that belief in God and the Bible and Jesus Christ as risen Savior and Lord is based on a sheer, uncertain, doubtful leap of faith. Such sheer decisionism that ignores evidence and argument is no better than the rage for absolute certainty that sets people up for a fall when they realize it is beyond human grasp. The word for belief based on such a mental leap of faith is "fideism," and it has nothing to commend it.

Yes, I believe in a debate with an atheist I can present better arguments for the existence of some Supreme Being than he or she can for that Being's nonexistence. But I know that's not what my audience in the debate is looking for; they come to see which debater can demolish the other and expect nothing less than proof as established by the Enlightenment (which I will discuss below). They also place the burden of proof on the believer in God and usually expect me to leave no possibility of doubt; if I admit some degree of doubt or uncertainty, they're more than disappointed. Most such audiences have little or no understanding of the frailty of human knowing. To them, "knowledge" is what can be proven; justified belief resulting in proper confidence rather than absolute proof is not knowledge. Unfortunately, too many conservative evangelicals have bought into that mentality. It's called the "evangelical enlightenment."

The "Evangelical Enlightenment"

Conservative evangelicals have too often succumbed to the rage for certainty that arose during the cultural revolution called the Enlightenment. It began in the mid-1600s with philosopher René Descartes, who was disturbed by the wars of religion that were devastating Europe at that time. He observed that whole populations were being killed or forced into exile over uncertain religious doctrines and practices and concluded that even religious belief should be based on reason rather than on revelation. (This laid the foundation for later deism, but many conservative Protestants also bought into this idea.) He sought one belief that he could prove and from there, he hoped, it would be possible to develop an entire system of philosophy, including theology, that would be based on proof rather than on faith.

One day Descartes decided to hide inside a large stove—a ceramic heating unit such as one still sees in the corners of some large European castle rooms. There he would not be deceived by his senses and, he hoped, he could find one item of knowledge beyond doubt. He started the process of cogitation by doubting everything he could doubt. The one thing he could not doubt was his own existence because to doubt requires existence. Thus, he came up with the famous first principle of foundationalism (the Enlightenment method of thinking): "I think, therefore I am" (*cogito ergo sum*). This first principle of Enlightenment foundationalist thinking has been parodied by many students and entertainers. During one episode of a nationally televised sitcom of the 1980s an air-headed young female character declared to her family that she was writing a paper for her college philosophy class with the title, "I Shop; Therefore I Am."

Descartes' first principle seemed self-evidently true. From there he attempted to use logic to demonstrate the existence of

God based on his own existence. The point is that a whole new way of thinking about knowledge—a Copernican revolution in thought—emerged from that stove that day. Ever since then philosophers and many theologians have thought it better to doubt everything first and then believe only what cannot be doubted (because it can be deduced directly or indirectly from an indubitable first principle). This was a major change from what had gone before especially in theology, where the first principle had always been "I believe in order that I may understand" (Anselm) or "faith seeking understanding." Now, because of Descartes and others like him, "understanding seeks faith." Facts come first and then faith.

This process was reflected in numerous evangelical Christian textbooks of theology throughout the nineteenth century and into the twentieth century. It is even found in the little "Four Spiritual Laws" booklet published by Campus Crusade for Christ and used as a witnessing tool by millions of conservative evangelicals. Christian apologetics grabbed onto it with titles like *Evidence That Demands a Verdict* (Authentic Lifestyle, 2004) and *No Doubt about It: The Case for Christianity* (B&H Publishing Group, 1997). (The latter is actually an excellent book, but when I used it as the text in an apologetics course it had a different title—*Reasonable Faith*. Later the publisher changed the title to one that reflects what most conservative evangelical Christians want and expect—proof beyond doubt of what they are taught at home and in church.)

An Alternative, Postmodern Approach to Christian Knowing

Two books revolutionized my thinking about all this certainty and faith stuff. I had my doubts about certainty for years and I felt guilty and ashamed because of them. But then I read a book by a colleague, Daniel Taylor, entitled *The Myth of Certainty: The Reflective Christian and the Risk of Commitment* (InterVarsity Press, 2000). It was and still is the most real book about faith and doubt I have ever read. I cannot recommend it highly enough. I would like to make it required reading for every evangelical Christian. The book is a thinly veiled and delightfully written account of the author's own experience teaching at a conservative evangelical college where a parade of chapel speakers and administrators gave students and faculty the impression that a real Christian will rise above all doubts and feel perfectly confident of the truth of evangelical Christian faith. Even honest questions were turned aside as unworthy of committed evangelicals; expressions of doubt were treated (as in my college experience) as sure evidence of flagging spirituality. Taylor recounts his own arrival at settled, confident, assured faith that is comfortable with not knowing the answers to all of life's ultimate questions and at least occasionally feeling doubts about even the most important doctrines of the church.

Another book that raised my consciousness about the reality of doubt and lack of absolute certainty in faith is by British ecumenical and evangelical missionary and theologian Lesslie Newbigin. Its title is *Proper Confidence: Faith, Doubt and Certainty in Christian Discipleship* (Eerdmans, 1995). It's a little book that packs a huge wallop! The book's thesis is that Western Christians have succumbed to an expectation of certainty that is simply unrealistic—even in science and philosophy. Faith pervades all knowing; to know is not to have absolute proof beyond any doubt but to believe with good reason. Perspective intrudes everywhere in knowing; even the hardest sciences involve faith in paradigms that control what is considered evidence. All knowing takes place within some grand narrative, some unifying scheme of truth that itself is beyond proving. Christianity is no different; like every other body of knowledge it involves belief without excluding reasons. The two go hand in hand in Christianity as in every other worldview and research project.

Newbigin's little book could be titled "Certainty Not." According to Newbigin, who is widely considered one of the most astute postmodern Christian thinkers, certainty is a modern quest and illusion; even Descartes' "I think, therefore I am" makes sense only to Western minds because many Asians don't believe in the self. (A basic belief of Buddhism is "no self.") And, of course, it is possible to question one's own objective existence as a doubting, questioning self. Newbigin, and many other postmodern Christians (including many evangelicals), believe we can and must learn to live without the kind of certainty modern, Western people seek.

But none of that means truth is unavailable to us. There's the big mistake especially conservatives make: the moment they hear a hint of doubt they assume truth is in question. Not so. I can believe in the truth of something while acknowledging that I could be wrong because I'm not God. And I can believe in something's truth while questioning it. To say that nothing is beyond doubt here and now, before heaven, is not to fall into skepticism; it is rather to admit that truth itself in all its perfection and completeness is transcendent to our puny, weak minds and that our finite perspectives always play a role in knowing.

Newbigin's book's title expresses the alternative to certainty well: "proper confidence." The popular Christian song "Blessed Assurance" says it as well. Even in the absence of perfect certainty and even in the presence of the possibility of doubt I can say with confidence and assurance "I believe!" In the next breath I might say, "Help thou my unbelief." But that doesn't take anything away from my confidence and assurance in the truth of Christ and his gospel; it only admits my finitude and fallenness.

Unfortunately, all too often, conservative evangelicals live in denial of these things and try to set up a standard of truth and certainty that is impossible. Speaking of conservatives, theologian Gary Dorrien writes in *The Remaking of Evangelical Theology* (Westminster John Knox, 1998):

> Evangelicals are prone to fret that everything will be lost if they have no ground of absolute certainty or no proof that Christianity is superior to Islam or Buddhism. This fear drives them to impose impossible tests on Christian belief. Inerrancy or the abyss! It also drives them to invest religious authority in a posited epistemological capacity that exists outside the circle of Christian faith. The truth of Christianity is then judged by rational tests that are not only external to Christian revelation but given authority over revelation. (201)

In other words, Dorrien complains, conservative evangelicals too often turn to rationalism (also known as foundationalism) to ground the certainty of what they believe. The problems are that it doesn't work and that it tries to base the truth of Christianity on secular authorities, such as "evidence that demands a verdict." The source and ground of Christian truth is rather the transforming, convincing power of God and the resulting faith. That doesn't mean there are no good reasons for faith; it only means that belief does not depend on rational proofs.

Not Certainty but Certitude

Many conservative evangelicals agree with that last sentence and eschew rationalistic Christianity. But they still seek a ground of certainty in experience. The "inner testimony of the Holy Spirit" (a phrase used much by the Reformer John Calvin) becomes the suprarational basis for certainty. External, rational proofs may not be valued by these conservatives, but certainty is just as important for them as for the rationalists. For example, whereas rationalist evangelicals base faith in the resurrection of Jesus (and ourselves) on historical evidences and arguments, these experientialist conservatives base it on direct, personal encounter and relationship with the living Christ through the Holy Spirit.

Pentecostals and many other revivalists are of this stripe. They love to sing, "You ask me how I know he lives; he lives within my heart." The rationalists would prefer to sing, "I know he lives because it's true beyond a reasonable doubt." But both groups of conservatives share in common a strong desire for and expectation of certainty that drives out all doubt.

The great Danish Protestant philosopher Søren Kierkegaard substituted *certitude* for certainty in Christian faith. He knew very well that absolute certainty that makes doubt and struggle and questioning impossible is beyond finite existence, and he detested the rationalism of Christian philosophers such as G. W. F. Hegel and his followers, who attempted to base the truth of Christianity on a rational system of philosophy. For Kierkegaard the true Christian is the one who commits himself or herself to God apart from certainty; the real "knight of faith" is the person who, like Abraham in the Old Testament, sets out plagued by doubt, taking risks for God without any proof or assurance that everything is safe and secure and settled.

Of course, Kierkegaard did not believe that the real Christian sits back in an easy chair questioning everything all the time; tired, chronic skepticism is not even in question here. Nor am I advocating that here. Instead, with Kierkegaard I'm advocating *certitude* over *certainty* in matters of Christian faith and belief. Certitude is the settled, inward assurance of faith; it believes without proofs and learns to live with doubts. To others this confident assurance without proof or certainty may appear to be something less than true spirituality because it may cause the person to furrow his or her brow in the presence of glib answers and clichés that are supposed to express doubtless faith. But it's more real and honest and sincere than the sunny, oblivious, pat answers of the many Dr. Panglosses of conservative evangelical folk religion. (Dr. Pangloss was Voltaire's mythical theologian who went around saying in the face of the worst calamities, "This is the best of all possible worlds, you know.")

So what of truth? How can a person search for and find truth without certainty as goal and finally possession? Conservatives worry that making certainty transcendent (not available here and now) inevitably causes people to give up the search for truth. It shouldn't, and they should stop worrying. A person can be thoroughly evangelical in his or her faith and at the same time admit to intellectual struggles and real doubts. And real evangelicals, whether conservative or not, will always be committed to truth and the search for it. Evangelical scholar Francis Schaeffer used to distinguish between "truth" with a little "t" and "Truth" with a large "T." The former is what we can grasp with some degree of certitude; the latter is what God alone knows. But that God knows it means that it exists, even if it is unavailable to us in all its perfection.

A nonconservative evangelical reserves to God the kind of ultimate grasp of Truth too many conservatives seek; and we attribute only to God the kind of unquestioning and doubtless knowing that too many conservatives claim to enjoy. In the meantime, lacking certainty but believing in Truth, we nonconservatives merrily (or sometimes not so merrily) continue our search for a greater grasp of reality and a better assurance and confidence than we have known so far. All the while we smile at our fellow evangelicals who think they have achieved that or hope to achieve it. And we cry quietly to ourselves when they belittle and berate those who admit it lies beyond their grasp or anyone's. We confess with the apostle Paul that now and until heaven we at best see the things of God as enigmas (one transliteration of the Greek word used in 1 Corinthians 13:12).

That's not because we lack any apprehension or assurance of them, but because our minds are incapable of full, certain knowledge of such great mysteries. But we have learned to live with mystery, ambiguity, and uncertainty without wallowing in chronic skepticism, like some of our liberal friends. Our honest motto is always, "I believe; help Thou my unbelief," and we reserve the right to raise honest and sincere questions about anything while continuing to believe what we are questioning.

CHAPTER 5

Taking the Bible Seriously without Literalism

One of the most common evangelical sermon illustrations when I was growing up in the 1950s and 1960s was about the home of eighteenth-century French skeptic Voltaire. Allegedly the house lived in by the man who scoffed at the Bible later became a Bible warehouse. Whether that's true or an "evangelegend" (religious urban legend) is hard to tell, but it well illustrates how evangelicals regard the Bible.

Evangelicals love the Bible. That's a given; everyone knows it to be true. It's part of the very definition of "evangelical" in America. (In Europe, "evangelical" often just means "Protestant.") Evangelicals are people of the book. Sometimes we are people of one book—a saying that simply means we love the Bible above all other books and consider it uniquely authoritative for believing and for practicing our faith.

Twentieth-century theologians Hans Frei and George Lindbeck, the two fathers of narrative and postliberal theology, talked about the Bible absorbing the world. They meant that for some Christians, and this would be especially true for evangelicals, the Bible provides the grand narrative, the great story of reality, through which we view and interpret the world around us and our lives within it. We do not bring the experienced world to the

Bible and interrogate the biblical story about God and humanity, nor do we read the Bible as referring to something outside itself such as universal human experience, which would make it a set of myths. Rather, evangelicals view the Bible as God's book and our book and we live our lives from it; it absorbs the world for us.

Nobody Takes the Whole Bible Literally

I can testify to that. When I was growing up in evangelical Christianity in America, the Bible was treated almost like a sacred object in our home and at our church. Especially my stepmother objected most strenuously if my brother or I placed any object on top of the Bible. Not all conservative evangelicals go that far. I've come to believe that such treatment of the physical paper, ink, and cover of the Bible is nearly idolatrous and sure evidence of folk religion. Nevertheless, virtually all conservative evangelicals revere the Bible and tend to interpret it as literally as possible. All evangelicals, whether conservative or not, hold the Bible as the uniquely inspired (God-breathed), written Word of God. But not all interpret it as literally as possible.

This matter of literal interpretation of the Bible used to be a watershed distinction between moderate evangelicals and fundamentalists; at least mainstream evangelicals thought that only their fundamentalist neighbors, the extreme fringe of the evangelical movement, took the whole Bible literally. In an evangelical seminary I was taught this signal difference between "us" and "them." I recognized that "them" included my family and church even though we didn't consider ourselves fundamentalists! Two comments are in order here. First, we were fundamentalists even though we didn't call ourselves that. My uncle, who was president of our denomination, called us "conservative evangelicals." In seminary I learned we were fundamentalists. I still think we were.

Second, many contemporary self-identified conservative evangelicals are really fundamentalists. In other words, whereas literal interpretation of the Bible was once tied especially with fundamentalism (maximal religious conservatism), it is now associated with conservative evangelicals in general because the nomenclature has changed. Fewer people want to be called fundamentalist; they now wish to be called conservative evangelicals and they have infiltrated the mainstream of evangelicalism in America under that label. But their theology is virtually unchanged, and they exercise a great deal of influence on the evangelical movement, resulting in a shift of the center to the right.

So what is this matter of taking the Bible literally? Why not take it literally? How can a person take the Bible seriously while not taking it literally? It's time to sort out some important issues. First, let's settle it that nobody takes all of the Bible literally. Even the most conservative fundamentalists know that when Isaiah 55:12 says the mountains and hills will sing for joy and the trees will clap their hands, it is meant metaphorically. This is poetry intended to describe the great joy of all creation at the second coming of Jesus Christ and the renewing of the earth by his power. Many more passages of the Bible could be adduced to show that it contains many figures of speech.

The trick, of course, is to know when something is meant figuratively and when it is meant literally. And even the term "literal" is a problem. What does that word mean? If something such as a word or a symbol refers to something other than itself, how can it be literal? Isn't there always some disconnect between the sign and what is signified? Ah, but now we wander into deep philosophical waters. My point is simpler: in spite of protestations to the contrary, few if any people take all of the Bible literally.

Literalistic Inconsistencies

Fundamentalists were known for much of the twentieth century as Christians who took the Bible as literally as possible. If it was possible to take a passage literally, it was to be taken literally. An often-repeated axiom of conservative Bible interpretation was that any passage should be interpreted "as literally as possible and as figuratively as necessary." Notice the strong preference for literal interpretation. Fundamentalists and many conservative evangelicals privilege literalism while acknowledging that some portions of Scripture must be recognized as figurative or symbolic. Moderate and progressive evangelicals called this woodenly literalistic interpretation; fundamentalist hermeneutics (Bible interpretation) seemed inflexible and flat.

That's what I was taught in an evangelical seminary in the 1970s; so were many other moderate evangelicals. For example, fundamentalists insisted on interpreting the days of the Genesis creation story as literal twenty-four-hour days. Many evangelicals did not; they agreed with the ancient church father Augustine that the Hebrew word *yom* could mean an indefinite period of time, an era or epoch. And we dared to notice that there are two creation accounts in Genesis—chapter 1 and then chapter 2. And they're not identical; chapter 1 spreads creation out over six days whereas chapter 2 seems to have it all happening on one day. So, many moderate evangelicals allowed that the first eleven chapters of Genesis might best be interpreted as what theologian Karl Barth called "saga"—a story about something that happened before recorded history recounted in a narrative with legendary features.

Few media people or others know about this because only those on the fringe of the evangelical movement tend to get any media attention. When those literalistic fundamentalists began to call themselves conservative evangelicals and were recognized as such by the media, moderate evangelicals who might have also welcomed the designation "conservative" began to have second thoughts. Today, most people think that all evangelicals believe in so-called "creationism," and creationism means not just that God created everything but that he did it in a literal week of six days of twenty-four hours each some ten thousand years ago. I've tried to tell people that I'm an evangelical who doesn't believe that and probably never has (at least since seminary). Many of them question my evangelical credentials. That's because of the media's adoption of "evangelical" for "biblical literalist."

So, if nobody takes the entire Bible literally and if fundamentalists or conservative evangelicals claim to take it literally, what is going on? What do they mean? This paradox—that fundamentalists claimed to interpret the Bible literally while admitting some of it is figurative—is one reason I became disillusioned with "biblical literalism" during and after college and dropped the phrase to describe my own way of taking the Bible seriously. But what did I mean before that? What do they who still claim to take the Bible literally mean? They mean that much of the Bible should be taken as literally as possible; the stories and references of the Bible that are not clearly poetic (like Isaiah 55) should be taken as referring to realities in time and space that could be captured by a digital camera or recording device. Any other interpretation, they say, dishonors Scripture and robs it of its truthfulness and authority. In this chapter I would like to suggest that this bias toward literalism is not essential for taking the Bible seriously and that one can be authentically evangelical and not privilege literal interpretation.

An example is the story of Jonah. What is the book of Jonah? Biblical literalists (and some moderates as well) insist that it is a historical account of real events that happened to a real person and that these events—including a sea monster (often translated "whale") swallowing Jonah—could have been recorded by video if the right technology had existed then. In other words, it is not a parable or legend or saga or myth. It is history. The Reformer Martin Luther could be a biblical literalist when he wanted to be (whereas other times he wasn't). He wrote that he found it difficult to believe that a whale swallowed a man, but if the Bible said a man swallowed a whale, he'd believe it. Biblical literalists applaud such statements.

Frankly, I'm not sure what the book of Jonah is or whether a whale (or sea monster) swallowed a man. My argument here is not that evangelicals (and others) should not take it literally; my argument here is that one can be an evangelical and not interpret it as a literal historical account. While the book can be interpreted literally as recounting events in history, it is not necessary to interpret it that way to take it seriously as God's Word.

The problem is that the same people who insist on interpreting Jonah literally often interpret other biblical passages that could be interpreted literally as figurative. For example, many biblical literalists (like Martin Luther) think that whereas Jonah was a real, historical person swallowed by a real, historical sea monster or whale, the "Antichrist" in the New Testament (especially in the book of Revelation) is a symbol for the bishop of Rome — the pope. Many conservative Protestants have agreed with Luther about that. A literal interpretation of that person, by contrast, would see him as a person to appear in the future who will dominate the world at the end of history and wage war against God's people. Christ will return to defeat and destroy him. Also, many conservative Christians who claim to take the Bible as literally as possible interpret the millennium mentioned three times in Revelation 20 as the entire time between Christ's first and second comings. For them it is the church age. But why? It is possible to interpret it literally as many do, so why not take it that way — as referring to a real thousand-year rule and reign of Christ on this earth after his Parousia (second coming).

Another example of this inconsistency is the way conservatives interpret Jesus' Sermon on the Mount in Matthew 5 – 7. There Jesus told his listeners to pluck out their right eyes and cut off their right hands if these body members caused them to sin (5:29 – 30). One early church father castrated himself based partly on a literal interpretation of that passage. But even in ancient times that was considered extreme; he was denied ordination by his bishop because of it. I have never met a fundamentalist or conservative evangelical who took Jesus' admonition in these two verses literally.

There is much else in the Sermon on the Mount they don't take literally. They consider these hard sayings of Jesus as figures of speech to underscore the seriousness of sin. And they interpret other seemingly impossible sayings of Jesus "counsels of perfection," which means ideals to strive for without thinking they can ever be achieved. An example is not resisting evil. Many, if not most, believers in a literal interpretation of the Bible believe that war is sometimes necessary — to resist evil. So, even those who claim to live by the hermeneutical rule "as literally as possible and as figuratively as necessary" don't. For some reason they interpret portions of the Bible figuratively that could be interpreted literally.

My point is that biblical literalism is a misleading concept; nobody believes every sentence in the Bible literally. Many who claim to be literalists and think others should be as well are selective and at times seemingly arbitrary in their literal and figurative interpretations. And many who do not claim to take the Bible entirely literally or even hold literalism as the norm take the Bible more seriously than some literalists! I'll come back to that later.

Let's return to Jonah as a case study of how it is possible to take the Bible seriously without taking it all literally. Conservative biblical scholars and theologians generally insist that Jonah is historical for two reasons. One is the rule that whatever can be taken literally should be taken literally. Admittedly, any good evangelical could interpret Jonah literally; nothing is impossible with God, including a whale or sea monster swallowing a man. The second reason is that the New Testament refers to Jonah as if he were a real person in history. If New Testament writers took Jonah literally, then so must we.

But some Bible-believing, evangelical scholars of the Old Testament believe there is good reason to think the book of Jonah was written as a "tract for the times." In other words, it doesn't fit the category of fable, nor is it myth or legend. But neither is it a literal description of historical events. It's closer to a parable. Even the most conservative Bible interpreters do not take Jesus' parables literally—even when they are not announced as parables. For example, the parable of the rich man and the poor man named Lazarus is not stated as a parable, but every conservative scholar I know considers it one. It could be interpreted as recounting actual events, so why not? Because it bears the marks of a parable. That is its literary genre.

So why take Jonah literally or insist that it must be taken literally? What if it displays marks of a parable? I'm no literary scholar, but I know that some evangelical scholars who firmly believe in the inspiration of the Bible happen to think the book of Jonah displays marks of a parable. I think they can take Jonah just as seriously as literalists do. The question is not so much whether it happened historically as whether it drives home its point, which is that God cares for all people, including those whom God's people consider outsiders to his kingdom.

My question to scholars and other people who treat Jonah figuratively rather than literally is "Why?" Why do they believe it isn't literal or historical but a parable? If the answer is because a whale or sea monster can't swallow a man and then spit him up whole and well, I have a problem with them. Some people interpret the Bible nonliterally who don't take it seriously, either! Taking the Bible seriously requires believing in miracles because the God of the biblical drama is a miracle-working God. Start with the resurrection of Jesus. Did it happen or not? If a person says it *could not* have happened because dead men don't come back to life, I argue that he or she is simply dismissing the main event of the biblical drama on which our salvation hangs! And they are saying God is unable to work miracles. If God exists, why couldn't he do miracles? I've never been able to understand people who say they believe in God but not in miracles.

However, if the person says he or she doesn't take Jonah literally or historically but as a parable for literary reasons and can convincingly show me that it is like Jesus' parables, I won't condemn him or her for that or label them as liberal. After all, I do believe Jesus told parables that are not to be taken literally or historically and some of them are not labeled "parable" in the text. So how can I be closed to interpreting Jonah as a parable? And what is lost by interpreting Jonah as a parable? What is lost by interpreting the six days of creation in Genesis 1 as eras or epochs of time? If a person interprets them that way only to accommodate to modern science, I do have a problem with that. But we know that the ancient church father Augustine thought they were indefinite periods of time and he didn't know anything about modern science. So, interpreting them as indefinite periods of time during which God created does not signal capitulation to secular science.

So how does one take the book of Jonah seriously without taking it literally? As an evangelical I believe it is part of the inspired canon of Scripture; it is not merely a human text without divine origin or authority. Necessary to being evangelical is accepting all of Scripture as inspired; it is not merely human but also divine in source and authority. That is a high view of Scripture. That's a watershed between evangelicals and nonevangelicals; evangelicals all attribute unique status as God's written Word to the Bible. They may disagree about the details, but they agree that the Bible is God's written, inspired, authoritative Word. Who doesn't believe in that? Well, many nonevangelical Protestants (and some Catholics as well) think of the Bible as existential truth cloaked in mythical form.

The great German New Testament scholar Rudolf Bultmann attempted to "demythologize" the Bible by showing that it is not about outer history at all; it is about human existence (self-understanding) as either authentic or inauthentic (as defined by existentialist philosophy). Liberal theologian Paul Tillich attempted to deliteralize the entire Bible and even God, whom he described as "the Ground of Being." Both Bultmann and Tillich interpreted the resurrection of Jesus Christ as the nonmiraculous rise of faith in the hearts and minds of the disciples after Jesus' death. According to them, Jesus is still dead. The tomb was not empty unless someone stole the body of Jesus. Why did they say these things? Because they began with a secular, naturalistic world view that ruled out miracles from the outset. Scientific naturalism (not to be confused with science) carried more weight than Scripture.

My personal opinion is that, in spite of the protestations of their followers, neither Bultmann nor Tillich took the Bible seriously. To them it was a great classic — fantastic literature. Many liberal Protestants view the Bible that way today. Evangelicals respectfully disagree; the Bible is God's book that carries ultimate authority for faith and life. But some of us believe it is not all meant to be taken literally *and* that the literal interpretation is not automatically privileged. And we admit that discerning the difference between that which is to be taken literally and that which is to be taken figuratively is not easy.

So, first of all, taking the Bible seriously means believing the book of Jonah, like the rest of the Bible, is God's written, inspired, and authoritative Word. Taking it seriously also means listening carefully to its "voice" and heeding it in life. The voice of God is speaking to us through it; we should adjust our living to its message whether or not we take it literally. Much more important than whether a sea monster swallowed a man and then spit him up is whether we love all people as God loves them—including those our tribe has always considered incorrigible and untouchable outsiders to the kingdom of God. And we must go to them with love and proclaim the gospel and pray for them to believe. That's taking Jonah seriously. If Jonah spurs one to such affection and action, it is being taken seriously whether or not a huge fish actually swallowed a human being.

Am I saying, then, that none of the Bible needs to be taken literally? Not at all. My family and I once were members of a Baptist church where the pastor told the Wednesday evening Bible study group that it doesn't matter if any of the Bible's stories actually happened; what matters is how they change lives. We left that church almost immediately. You might be thinking the pastor's words describe this chapter quite well. You'd be wrong. My point is not at all that none of the Bible is historical, but I am arguing that some of it can be history-like without necessarily being historical. I have used Jonah as an example of a biblical character who may not have lived and yet can serve as a great example to us. But Abraham, for example, is a different matter. I have talked to people who claim to take the Bible seriously but who do not believe Abraham ever existed; to them he is a mythical or legendary figure in the Old Testament. That's harder to accept than Jonah! Abraham is a (if not the) key covenant figure in the Bible other than Jesus himself. With whom did God make a covenant to bless the nations of the world if not with someone named Abraham? The historicity of Abraham is crucial to the biblical drama in a way the historicity of Jonah is not.

Discerning the Difference

How can we discern the difference between that which is to be taken literally and that which is to be taken figuratively in the Bible? Space prohibits a complete exploration of that question here. Entire volumes have been written about it. It is probably the biggest question in the discipline called biblical hermeneutics—interpreting Scripture. Nobody can provide a litmus test that neatly and clearly demonstrates a passage to be literal or figurative. With that caveat in mind, I'll take the plunge and provide some pointers.

First, what kind of literature is the passage or entire book? And what does this entail for the interpretation of the passage? This is where the ordinary layperson is going to have to rely partly on trusted biblical scholars. Since they don't always agree, however, the layperson and pastor are going to have to make a decision. Hopefully it is an informed decision and not a shot in the dark. Start with something everyone agrees on—such as that Jesus' parables are nonliteral literature that should be taken seriously.

Jesus' parable of the good Samaritan is well known and nobody (to the best of my knowledge) considers it something that really happened. It could have happened, of course, but whether or not it did happen is irrelevant to the point of the story; about that virtually everyone agrees. Why? Because it has the marks of a parable—a literary device shaped as a story with a single main theological point. It's not an allegory, which is another kind of literature altogether. An allegory is a story in which most of the elements refer to something else. A biblical example of allegory is the apostle Paul's use of the Old Testament women Sarah and Hagar to refer to the gospel and the law (Galatians 4:21–31).

The parable of the Good Samaritan has one main point—God's people are expected to be like the kindly outcast from God's people (Samaritans were disdained by Jews) and be good neighbors providing for those in need. They are not to be like the Jewish leaders who passed by the man without caring for him. There may be theological depths to the story not plumbed here, but the point is clear—the parable stands on its own two feet as a gospel message in a metaphor whether it ever actually happened or not. What would it add to the impact of the story if it had happened? Nothing. It could have happened. That's the point. It is history-like without being historical. About this almost all conservative Christians agree.

Second, look at the theological point of the book or passage and ask whether anything crucial to the biblical drama and its theological message is lost if the book or passage is interpreted nonliterally. Does the biblical drama require that this person or event be historical? Does it require that the command or saying be taken literally? What happens to the overall biblical narrative if it is interpreted figuratively rather than historically or literally? I would argue that Abraham is crucial to the biblical drama; to deny his historicity is to cut the heart out of the story of God's covenant with human beings. The same is true of later biblical characters such as Moses and David. Whether everything that is recorded about them is literally true is another matter, but that they existed and lived their lives before God as told in the stories about them is more than important to the overall biblical message. Abraham, Moses, and David are historical and theological characters; in these cases the two are inextricably intertwined.

These two considerations can go a long way toward helping a Bible reader and interpreter decide whether a story or saying is literally true or to be taken nonliterally. It is important to understand, of course, that "truth" can be conveyed nonliterally. Many people miss this important point in this discussion even as they know it in daily life. A good movie such as *Gone with the Wind* can convey a powerful and true message about the strength of a determined and persevering person. The old legend of George Washington and the cherry tree conveys a message about honesty even if it never really happened.

The early church fathers knew this well. Most of them interpreted the Bible allegorically—something that embarrasses many modern conservative evangelicals. Most of the church fathers thought the Bible has layers of meaning. The least important meaning is the historical one. The second least/most important meaning is ethical or moral. The most important meaning is theological. Thus, for example, the great church father Origen believed that the entire Bible was dictated by God but at the same time he believed much of it is not literally true. And the literal, historical truth of it is relatively unimportant. I disagree with Origen, but it's interesting to note that church fathers found great meaning and truth in nonliteral interpretation of biblical texts.

How to Take the Bible Seriously

So, once again, what does it mean to be evangelical and take the Bible seriously without always taking it literally? An evangelical is someone who fervently and passionately displays the four or five characteristics outlined and explained in this book's introduction: *biblicism* (loves the Bible and regards it as God's authoritative, inspired, written Word), *conversionism* (has had a "born again" experience and believes something like that is the necessary beginning of a truly Christian life), *crucicentrism* (piety and devotion centered around the cross of Jesus Christ and the atonement for sins provided there), and *activism* (evangelism, missions, social transformation). A fifth characteristic may be *respect for the great tradition of Christian doctrine.* (I added that to the more standard and widely accepted four marks of evangelical faith.)

My point in this chapter is that it is possible to be authentically and fully evangelical and not take all of the history-like parts of the Bible literally as historical. It is not that a literalistic interpretation of the Bible is wrong, but I argue that one can be authentically evangelical without practicing it. The common evangelical approach to the Bible is not tied to interpretation but love for it and obedience to its message. At the same time, there are approaches to the Bible that are inconsistent with authentic evangelical Christianity, such as Bultmann's demythologizing method. Taking the Bible seriously is not consistent with imposing on it a modern, naturalistic worldview so that its message becomes something only about human existence. Taking it seriously means struggling to hear and obey its message as one that comes genuinely from God. That requires interpreting some of it—but not all of it—and even parts usually considered historical and literally true by most conservatives as perhaps not such in all evangelicals' eyes.

CHAPTER 6

BEING RELIGIONLESS
WITHOUT SECULARISM

Many contemporary young Christians and other young people are disillusioned with religion; it's common to hear a person say, "I'm not religious, but I am spiritual." Many conservative evangelicals scoff at this, but there may be something to it. Of course, all depends on what is meant by "religious." I'll come back to that later.

When people say, "I'm not religious, but I am spiritual," many conservative Christians immediately assume they mean one of two things. Either they belong to some spiritual or occult practice (like a New Age sect or some form of Eastern spirituality) or they are really secular but riding the popular wave of "spirituality." Conservative Christians, including many evangelicals, resist any separation of religion from authentic spirituality. To them "religion" is a positive thing, especially if it is related to organized Christianity. Or they may not talk about being religious, but their behavior betrays a deep commitment to religion and religious forms of life.

The Problem with "Religion"

Here I raise the question whether it is possible to discard "religion" altogether and still be authentically Christian. Most conservative evangelicals would say no. Most observers of the evangelical movement would laugh at the idea. They consider evangelicals the most religious of all Americans. My thesis in this chapter is that, as strange as it may sound, a person may be more authentically evangelical by being less religious insofar as "religion" signifies commitment to traditional religious forms of life as they are commonly found and practiced in America. Being evangelically Christian and being religious do not necessarily go together; you can be nonreligious and nevertheless be truly evangelical.

Some readers might think I'm just out to shock readers. They might think back to the 1960s "radical theologians," who spoke and wrote about "religionless Christianity." They often appealed to the great German theologian and martyr Dietrich Bonhoeffer, who wrote about religionless Christianity and "holy worldliness" in his *Letters and Papers from Prison* (Macmillan, 1962). But the 1960s radical theologians (some of who were self-proclaimed "Christian atheists") distorted Bonhoeffer's ideas and tried to secularize Christianity. That's the furthest thing from my mind here; by no means do I intend to secularize evangelicals. My interest is in exploring how it might be possible to be more evangelical without being religious while at the same time avoiding secularity or New Age spirituality.

That seems counterintuitive; I suspect most people's initial reaction is one of suspicion. I hope at least to open the minds of evangelicals (and observers of evangelicals) to that possibility for the sake of the church's mission in the world. Today, religiosity turns off many people, including many evangelical young people, to the gospel. And I think it dulls the sharp edge of real Christianity by blunting it with layers and coats of tradition and comfort.

I should define "religion" at this point. I hold a Ph.D. degree in religious studies from a major American university, and I can tell you with assurance that "religion" has no definite definition. You can look it up in a dictionary, but the definitions found there will at best cover some of the term's semantic range but not all of it. One noted scholar of religion defines "religion" as any "means of ultimate transformation." In other words, it does not have to include belief in any God or gods or spirits as most people assume.

Buddhism, for example, is a religion (or collection of religions) without God or gods. (It's true that some forms of Buddhism talk about gods, but they don't mean gods in the Western sense. They mean "bodhisattvas," which are personalized manifestations of the experience of enlightenment. Classical Buddhist "theology" [if it can be called that] does not teach about a God or gods in any sense analogous to Judaism, Christianity, or Islam.) "Religion" is a flexible and possibly essentially contested concept. So, I have to define my meaning of it and hope that readers can agree that what I mean by religion in this chapter is somewhat close to what they and/or most people in contemporary American life mean by it.

Here's what I mean by "religion": a fairly formalized, institutionalized, relatively tradition-bound worship and spirituality. I know that's how many younger people, including many evangelical youths, understand it. This is what comes to their minds when they hear the word "religion": "churchiness." I've lived in both Texas and Minnesota. They are very different cultures within one country, so I'll describe here how religion is generally understood in both.

An Alternative to Being "Secular" or "Religious"

In Minnesota, like much of the northern tier of states, religion is largely identified with going to and participating in an organized, institutionalized church. To most people that's either Catholic or Lutheran. So, being religious is being personally, voluntarily affiliated with a church and its traditions. Being nonreligious means being secular or New Age — which usually means an individualized spirituality made up of bits and pieces of Eastern religions, the occult, and esoteric beliefs such as reincarnation.

Many young people in Minnesota feel trapped between these two identities; they don't want to be religious in the sense of churchiness, but neither do they want to be secular or New Age. Many of these are evangelicals whether they call themselves that or not. But to many of them "evangelical" is inextricably linked to "religiosity," so they don't consider themselves evangelical. To them, and to other nonconservative evangelicals, religion signifies traditional, organized, institutionalized, and formalized spirituality. It seems like putting God in a box. It resists risk and change. It's more about preserving institutions than mission; it's often an exercise in "us versus them" with regard to the world outside of and around religious organizations and institutions such as churches and religious schools. So, in Minnesota younger evangelical Christians gather in new, emerging, experimental Christian communities that are intentionally nonreligious. They have names like Solomon's Porch, Spirit Garage, and House of Mercy.

In Texas the situation is somewhat different. The culture is more overtly religious and even Christian. Secularism is not nearly as popular or normal in Texas (or most of the South) as in Minnesota (and large swaths of the North). Religion pervades everything; it's not unusual to hear television personalities such as news anchors encourage viewers to attend church. And religion in Texas revolves around institutionalized churches. Many people think they are authentically religious and Christian merely because they grew up in and never left church.

People in the South talk about church a great deal, but it's not as common to hear about Jesus. Being Baptist or Catholic is often more important than being Christian. My wife belonged to a women's book club composed mainly of faculty wives of a Christian university. She found a genuine, heartfelt, and sincere love for their churches among the women but a reluctance to talk about personal relationships with God or Jesus. They were very religious (which is not necessarily a bad thing) but not particularly warmly evangelical even though many of them would consider themselves conservative Christians.

In Texas as in Minnesota (and much of the country) younger Christians from evangelical backgrounds are becoming disillusioned with "churchianity," which is for them a synonym for "religion." So they gather in small groups, seeking an authentic expression of Christianity apart from institutionalized, tradition-bound, and inward-looking churches. These emerging, nonreligious churches are usually evangelical in ethos, and they experiment with new forms of worship and community life often drawn from ancient Christian sources and all kinds of art.

But these so-called emerging, youth-oriented churches aren't the only expressions of religionless Christianity in Texas or elsewhere. There's a church (if you can call it that) in Waco, Texas, where I live, that nobody would consider religious. This unusual Christian community is called Church under the Bridge; it meets on Sunday mornings under an overpass on Interstate 35 through Waco. The traffic between Dallas/Fort Worth and Austin/San Antonio buzzes and blares overhead as two or three hundred people gather to sing praises to God, enjoy Christian fellowship, and hear someone talk conversationally about what Jesus can do in a person's life. Often there are testimonies from homeless men and women and from people still in the grip of addiction but seeking the freedom Christ provides.

This church is a ministry of Mission Waco — a thriving Christian development and empowerment organization that eschews formal religious trappings such as requiring people receiving help to attend a worship service or read a tract. Church under the Bridge appears to outsiders to be a disorganized mess; there's no liturgy, formal tradition, or obvious leadership with authority. And the congregation is as diverse as the Waco community. I often ask my students, "If Jesus came to Waco, where would he attend church?" Most of them think a moment and reply, "Church under the Bridge." Then why aren't more churches like it in some way?

Another nonreligious Waco congregation is ACTS Christian Fellowship, which bills itself as the "church without walls." It is officially Baptist but functionally nondenominational. The church conducts Sunday morning worship in a building and has the usual children's, women's, and men's ministries. But it is a church all about mission; the congregation and ministry team wrap the entire church life around the physically and spiritually needy people of the Waco community. In 2007 it voted to sell its rather nonchurchly building on the edge of town and move downtown near the city's largest homeless shelter. Most churches move the other direction; ACTS Christian Fellowship breaks the trend by moving from the suburbs into urban blight and decay to be salt and light there.

These Christians have no intention of lording it over folks or telling them how to behave or simply evangelizing them. Their intention is to be the presence of Jesus Christ in the midst of the dying world. To use a 1960s phrase that became old and tiresome then but may now be ready for a new lease on life: this church "allows the world to set the church's agenda." That's holy worldliness in Bonhoeffer's terms.

My purpose in describing these churches is not to say that every church should imitate them. What I'm trying to point out is that it is okay to take risks with nontraditional forms of church life; it is okay to buck traditions, institutionalism, and the club-like atmosphere of so much conservative religious life in America and go out on limbs for Jesus. Are there dangers in that? Of course; every risk includes a danger. But without risks people and communities tend to settle into apathy and lethargy and eventually die spiritually if not organizationally.

An Example of a "Religious Church"

Perhaps I can give you an example of a church that wallowed in religion by refusing to let go of traditions and take some risks. One of the most conservative churches I've ever been part of was also theologically liberal. That's the irony; a church can be conservative to the core in terms of its religiosity and yet be theologically liberal in the sense of accommodating to modernity in its beliefs. Many years ago I was youth pastor of one of the finest Christian congregations I have ever known; they welcomed my wife and me into their midst with open arms even though we were not of that denomination. And they gave us unqualified support as we ministered to their teenagers. We loved those kids and still stay in touch with them occasionally. But this church was stuck in religion; it had no energy to take risks and move into the twenty-first century and adapt to its neighborhood. We could see the church dying before our eyes. Surprisingly, years later the church is still there and its physical facilities are nicer than ever. Someone died and left lots of money to the church to refurbish them.

Like so many other congregations, this one functioned much like a religious club. There was no mentality of being missional. The beautiful brick buildings and perfectly cut lawn stood in the midst of a neighborhood in dramatic transition — from an upper class, white, Southernly, genteel suburb to an inner city, poverty-stricken ghetto populated largely by immigrants from Latin America. Many of them did not speak English and probably did not have legal residency in the United States. I spoke often and warmly of the need to adapt to the neighborhood, but the good people of that church were either afraid or so in love with their traditions (or both) that they couldn't do it.

For example, when our church hosted the annual Vacation Bible School held jointly by four Protestant congregations of different denominations, the leadership forbade me to go around the neighborhood randomly inviting children to VBS. I was shocked and did it anyway. Then I got in trouble because one little Hispanic child broke a window accidentally; in the process he cut his hand and needed stitches. His parents were nowhere to be found. The church had to pay for the window and the child's stitches at the local emergency room. That week I received a lot of frowns from my congregants.

Were they bad people? Not at all. They were very religious people. To them the church buildings and grounds and their finances and their worship (no Spanish, please!) meant more than taking risks to reach the neighborhood. I know this church is not alone; many if not most American congregations are like it. Does that mean such churches should be abolished or simply left behind by missional Christians? Not at all; they deserve our love and respect and patience. But if they refuse to let go of religion in order to become genuinely evangelical (which necessarily includes being missional), they probably should be lovingly abandoned.

"Missional" Versus "Religious"

Back to religion. What's distinctively "religious" about the churches so many young Christians and missional evangelicals are leaving behind for new experiments in being church that might be called "nonreligious"? It comes down to resistance to change and love of tradition and comfort within a religious/spiritual context. To most people today, "religion" means traditional church life with all its trappings that are closed to new impulses, risks, and forward-looking missional movement. You may be thinking "That's not how I understand 'religion.'" Fine. But many people in America in the early twenty-first century do think of religion that way. And it is closely tied with being conservative — culturally, socially, doctrinally, ecclesiastically (structure and leadership), and liturgically (worship). Being "religious" is having a critical mass of these conservative characteristics and resisting change in or from them.

So how does a person or church or other organization become authentically evangelical without being religious? Is religionless evangelical faith possible? Some people say, "Surely not. Religion and evangelical go together inextricably in the popular American mind." I'm not prepared to consent to that; it seems to me a category confusion — especially when "religion" is defined as I have defined it here (which I'm convinced is the way many younger people think of it).

The answer will not be simple or easy. First, let's review what "evangelical" means. As I explained in the introduction, anyone (individual or group) is evangelical who displays all five of these characteristics: *biblicism, conversionism, crucicentrism, activism,* and *respect for the Great Tradition of Christian doctrine.* Some people (especially some conservative theologians) will consider this too minimal; they'll want to pack a lot of dogmas into the "evangelical." I think my five hallmarks are sufficient and so do a number of other evangelical scholars and scholars of evangelicalism.

So how can a person be a religionless evangelical without being secular? "Secular" means living life without God. It doesn't necessarily entail atheism or even agnosticism, but it does entail a kind of functional atheism—God is privatized and not central to life. Can a person be religionless and not secular? That's counterintuitive at best; many people probably think the two go together. I don't. I believe authentic Christianity is religionless but not secular in the least. And I consider evangelical faith the most authentic form of Christianity. What would a religionless but not secular evangelical faith look like? Not necessarily like any of the experimental churches I mentioned earlier but far from the tradition-bound religious clubs that exclude their neighbors and refuse to be missional or in touch with the world around them.

On Taking Risks

A religionless evangelical individual or church refuses to be bound by traditions. Much more important than being traditional and much more important than people's comfort zones is being the presence of Jesus Christ in the middle of the world, which often means in the middle of decaying, urban centers of cities. Even smaller cities now have such crowded neighborhoods that are crime-ridden and poverty-stricken. Most churches, including evangelical churches, have abandoned them. Most evangelicals (with the exception of African Americans and Hispanic people) have moved out to the suburbs. That's because they—the churches and the people—did not want the world around them to shape their church life; they wanted to preserve their traditions and continue their Sunday morning religious club meetings oblivious to the horrors of America's inner cities. In spite of speeches to the contrary, that is not authentic evangelicalism.

Where were the first churches? The New Testament indicates they were in the largest pagan cities of the Roman empire. Paul's two letters to the Corinthian Christians make undeniably clear that the Christians there were surrounded by the moral decay and false religions of that Greek city. There is no hint that they should build walls to keep the ungodly out or be uninvolved in their cities' lives. Being authentically evangelical today requires missional, risk-taking contact with the neighborhoods where the gospel is not being lived out, both by preaching and by making a difference in people's lives.

Authentic evangelical Christianity may respect traditional Christian beliefs, but it is willing to take risks and does not resist change. I'm not advocating change for change's sake, of course, but risks and change to stay relevant to the contemporary world. By "relevant" I don't mean "accommodating" to culture, for evangelicals know they have a message that the surrounding culture doesn't have. By "relevant" I mean in touch with contemporary social realities. For example, in the name of being conservative and religious, too many evangelical churches shun everything about today's youth culture. They try to shelter young people from it without knowing much about it.

Take, for example, rap music. Many young males (and some females) are drawn to rap music as a genre. Conservative adult Christians who enjoy jazz may forget that it was at one time considered controversial for many of the same reasons as rap. I'm not advocating that evangelical churches uncritically embrace all rap music; some of it is clearly anti-Christian and anti-human (to say nothing of anti-women!). But I do think a relevant, contemporary, religionless evangelicalism should not simply reject the entire musical genre.

More often rap music is rejected because of stereotypes about it as a musical genre; it is believed to promote drugs and killing. Some of it does. But much Country and Western music glorifies drunkenness and "womanizing" (adultery). Do evangelicals reject this type of music for that reason? Not often. Can rap music be adapted for worship? Conservatives recoil with horror at the suggestion. Personally, I don't like rap music. But that doesn't mean I should fight against it if my younger brothers and sisters are finding it helpful and enjoyable and can adapt it to their faith without compromising the gospel.

What about secular literature and movies and dance? Can these be incorporated into worship, Bible study, and Christian mission? Why not? But that's not usually considered a religious thing to do, and many conservative evangelicals resist it. Some younger Christians gather to watch secular movies to discuss gospel themes in them. Our church conducted a six-week study on Wednesday evenings, taking a different major Hollywood film each week and discussing Christian themes in them. Some groups of nonreligious Christians are using secular literature such as poetry and novels to stimulate their faith. These are not replacing the Bible but being treated as vehicles of common grace, through which some light of God might shine.

Some risk-taking evangelical churches are experimenting with drama and dance in worship. Often, conservative religious folks protest but fail to realize that God can use all of our senses to stimulate and inspire us. Conservative religious folks are too focused on words; they tend to forget about the power of symbols to speak to and transform people's lives.

These are just a few examples of how churches can become more relevant to culture without compromising the gospel. In and through all of this, of course, must shine the gospel as it is found in the Bible. And traditional doctrinal teachings should not be abandoned even if they are questioned and revised in the light of better understanding of Scripture.

My message in this chapter is not radical or new. Older evangelical readers probably remember a popular 1967 Christian film called *The Gospel Blimp*. It was based on a story written by evangelical author Joseph Bayly. The gospel blimp was an evangelistic tool cooked up by a group of Christians; it would float above the city displaying and blaring gospel messages to the people down below. But one man originally associated with the project found a better tool of evangelism — much to his colleagues' dismay. He befriended his neighbors and attended their cookouts that probably (although the story and film don't say) had beer. The man who befriended his neighbors won more people to Christ by his seemingly religionless methods than the very religious evangelism of the gospel blimpers! Joseph Bayly was an astute critic of religion; he saw the need for a religionless evangelicalism that was not in any way secular and portrayed it in his stories.

No "Secular Christianity"

So how is religionless evangelicalism not secular? Some readers undoubtedly fear that any step away from formal religion automatically means a step toward (if not a fall into) secularity. Not at all. Evangelical faith necessarily includes God at the center of life; there is no question of a secular evangelicalism. That is not to say, of course, that evangelical faith has to reject everything that seems secular! I once knew a Bible college president who discarded all the records of "secular" (non-sacred) music from the library. That's not at all necessary to authentic evangelical faith!

But placing God at the center is necessary. An evangelical Christian's life revolves around God, and when God is at the center of life he may very well call an evangelical individual or group to "die" (using Bonhoeffer's words from *The Cost of Discipleship*) to tradition and step forth taking risks for the love that God has for the seemingly godless world. And that may feel much like leaving religion behind and becoming religionless. But it will not be leaving God or Jesus or the Holy Spirit or miracles out of the picture, so it will not feel like becoming secular, for secularism tends to marginalize God and rule out anything supernatural. In an ironic twist, "religion" has become somewhat secular because it has tended to push God out of the center and replace him with traditions and comfort and institutions. A simple reading of the Bible shows clearly that the real God calls people to take risks for him, and he works miracles as they step forth in faith away from comfort zones — including religious ones — to follow him.

What about doctrines? Religion is often closely associated with strong doctrinal beliefs. Does religionless evangelicalism cast off doctrines? Absolutely not. It is not doctrines that are religious (in this chapter's sense of "religious") but the attitude that doctrines are more important than experiencing God in transforming ways. Too often religion is an information delivery system whereas authentic evangelical Christianity is about personal and communal transformation by God's Spirit, bringing people to Jesus Christ with repentance and the resulting miracle of regeneration — the new life that loves God and the things of God and people.

Evangelical faith inevitably leads to faithful interpretation of the Bible in the light of conversion, including the Spirit's regeneration of people. That inevitably gives rise to doctrines. But doctrines are not the center; they are intended to be ministerial (serving as servants) rather than magisterial (serving as masters). In other words, doctrines serve people rather than vice versa. Doctrines express a Christian community's consensus about right interpretation of the Bible in the light of experience; they go wrong when they are enshrined as unquestionable authorities that enslave people's minds and forbid all doubt or questioning.

Religionless evangelicalism will have doctrines, but it will approach them differently — with a different attitude that holds them lightly and keeps them open to reconsideration and revision (see chapter 1). Secularity would enter this picture if some culture like "modernity" or "postmodernity" were allowed to become a major source or norm of Christian doctrine, but as long the Word of God is what gives rise to doctrine and norms, there is no hint of secularism.

In sum, then, "religionless evangelicalism" is focused on being missional more than informational. It is open to revision of traditional beliefs and practices in light of fresh and faithful interpretations of God's Word. It is willing to take the risk of departing from everything considered "religious" by most people in order to reach the secular world for Jesus Christ. To many conservatives, it may appear secularized or "worldly," but to religionless evangelicals it will appear as going where Jesus would go to be truly with the people of this world.

CHAPTER 7

TRANSFORMING CULTURE
WITHOUT DOMINATION

The class was discussing Christian social ethics within the context of separation of church and state. Most students expressed the idea that Christians must be careful not to impose Christian beliefs and values on everyone. After all, they said, what if another religion tried to impose its beliefs and values on us? Wouldn't we object? The majority nodded in agreement.

But one student demurred. When asked to explain, he argued that since Christianity is true and other religions are false, Christians have a duty to try to mold and shape society according to Christian beliefs and values to the exclusion of other influences. "Christians should take over and rule," he explained. "After all, if we don't, somebody else will." The class fell into a virtual uproar over the issue of how Christians should best try to transform society without necessarily "Christianizing culture."

One of the problems with being "conservative" in today's cultural and religious climate is the long shadow of the so-called Religious Right, composed mainly of conservative evangelical social and political activists. In the popular American mind, to the person on the street, "conservative evangelical" (if not just "evangelical") has come to mean a person who wishes to use political means to make people behave. The old adage "you can't legislate morality" is the attitude many express toward the Religious Right. Conservative evangelicals are perceived as people who want to criminalize behavior inconsistent with the Bible or with Christian values and principles.

Of course, those who identify themselves with the Religious Right (whether calling themselves that or not) protest and sometimes rightly so. They really want to return America to a time when basic decency was taken for granted and indecency was punished in some way. In our postmodern, pluralistic society, however, that begs the question, "Whose decency and whose indecency? Who defines these concepts? Is there a social consensus?" Sometimes it seems as if conservative evangelicals don't care if there is a social consensus about an issue; they just want to enforce their vision of decency on everyone.

Conservative Christians and Conservative Politics

To a certain extent the above is a caricature of what politically active evangelical social conservatives really want. But to some extent at least, that perception is reality, and it is difficult to remove and discard, largely because the media identifies the category "evangelical" as the Religious Right. Personally, I'm not ready to concede that perception as reality just yet. As I have emphasized before, I and many other evangelicals insist on keeping that label, but we are ready to give up on being labeled conservative. It is nearly impossible to distance oneself from the Religious Right and still call oneself a conservative evangelical.

I should admit up front, however, that there is a certain amount of distortion in this popular perception. What the media and most people who buy into this identification don't realize is that many conservative evangelicals really have no interest in politics or in changing society into their own image. Many conservative evangelicals are still minding their own business and showing little to no concern for Christianizing the social order (to borrow an old phrase from the Social Gospel movement of the early 1900s).

Most of these people are in Bible-believing, evangelistic churches that practice social conservatism in their own family lives without engaging in any political movement to enforce it on others. They don't drink alcohol, but they're not in favor of prohibition; they don't engage in extramarital sex, but they don't want to criminalize it. They care about the behavior of society, but they see the solution to bad behavior lying in conversion and not in coercion by law. The media largely overlook these evangelicals; they are conservative but they don't fit the stereotype of angry Puritans trying to put people who don't obey the Bible in stocks!

The popular image of all conservative Christians as narrow-minded, legalistic, political activists is largely a figment of the media's collective imagination. That has been proven beyond doubt by Andrew Greeley and Michael Hout in their stereotype-busting sociological portrait of conservative Christians entitled *The Truth about Conservative Christians: What They Think and What They Believe* (University of Chicago Press, 2006). Greeley is one of the best-known sociologists of religion in America; Michael Hout is also a sociologist of some renown. In their book these two authors explode many myths about conservative Christians, including that all evangelicals are interested in criminalizing abortion and homosexuality. The statistics they marshal demonstrate that to be a myth. They use a thirty-year study of the religious, social, and political attitudes of American Christians to show that those identified as conservative (by their denominational affiliations) differ only negligibly from those identified as "mainline" on most questions having to do with politics and ethics. For example, most conservative Christians are not against all abortions; most of them regard some abortions as ethically justified and many do not think any abortions should be criminalized.

The Truth about Conservative Christians shows conclusively that a person can be evangelical without belonging to the Religious Right or any movement intent on taking over or controlling government in order to enforce Christian beliefs and values on all citizens. (The authors tend to equate "evangelical" with "conservative Protestant," but the upshot of their analysis of the data is that many people in that combined category are not very different from so-called mainline Christians in their social and political attitudes.) Nevertheless, there is some truth to the perception that conservative evangelicals were instrumental in the Republican takeover of government at the time of Ronald Reagan's election and have exercised considerable, if not determining, influence in every election since then. Enough conservative evangelicals are politically active for conservative causes to justify the perception of the movement as tilting toward the right and even desiring something akin to a theocracy in America.

The evidence for that claim is necessarily anecdotal. Almost nobody admits to wanting an American theocracy (a government controlled by a church or religious leaders). That some want it nevertheless is apparent to anyone who watches and listens carefully to the pronouncements of leaders of the Religious Right, most of whom are self-identified conservative evangelicals. The leadership of the Southern Baptist Convention, the largest Protestant denomination in America, walks almost lockstep along that front. Year after year the messengers (delegates) to the SBC annual convention pass resolutions sounding much like calls to arms for politically active conservative Christians. (Of course, by "call to arms" I don't literally mean weapons of deadly force but political means of legislating moral behavior.) Almost everyone knows somebody who votes only for "Christian" candidates, who are almost always conservative Republicans.

Conservative Evangelicals and the Religious Right

In this chapter, then, I am dealing not with all conservative evangelicals but only with those who do want to take over American culture for Christ using political power. Many of them never attend political party caucuses or vote in primaries or national elections and some of them don't belong to any political party, but they all favor transforming American culture by legislating Christian ethics, which means criminalizing what they consider immoral behavior.

I live in Texas, one of the most conservative states in America as well as one of the most religious ones. A few years ago the United States Supreme Court struck down a Texas law that criminalized sodomy even between consenting adults in the privacy of their own homes. Even many moderate Baptists who didn't affiliate or identify with the Religious Right were outraged. Why? Because, like many conservative Christians in America, they assume that indecent behavior should be illegal and defined by religious and not secular or pagan people. I take it that that view is common among conservative evangelicals in America.

I often find myself alone when I oppose laws criminalizing sexual acts between consenting adults and capital punishment and banning all abortions. I stand out in my context, at least, as something of an odd duck. People have trouble believing I'm an evangelical. Don't all evangelicals support the American government's foreign military adventures? Don't they all demonstrate against abortion or support those who do? Don't they all condemn homosexuals to hell? Hardly. But the problem is that we evangelicals who don't fit that popular image get no press coverage; people hardly know we exist. And because of the journalistic use of "evangelical" many people simply won't believe we are authentic evangelicals!

I want to make the case that a person can be authentically evangelical without desiring to transform culture by using government to legislate Christian ethics. One can be evangelical without sympathizing with the Religious Right. One can also be mainline Protestant without sympathizing with the Religious Left (such people are also ignored by the media). The Religious Left isn't as organized as the Religious Right and its leaders tend to play down the connection between their religious convictions and their advocacy of certain governmental policies. But to the extent that they want to make policy based solely on their Christian convictions, they too are seeking a theocracy and have no ground to criticize the Religious Right.

Again, we must revisit the meaning of "evangelical." Some readers may have jumped directly to this chapter without reading the introduction and may have missed my meaning of the term. Who is an evangelical? Well, I am still tempted to say an evangelical is anyone who admires Billy Graham. But, of course, that won't wash because some people admire him without agreeing with his message. But the very mention of Billy Graham here helps make my point. Although he has been a friend of several presidents, Graham has never engaged in a political crusade or advocated legislation of Christian behavior. Yet he stands as the undisputed paragon of evangelicalism. If the evangelical movement in America has anything close to a pope, it's Graham. Fortunately, he doesn't pontificate or speak for all evangelicals, but virtually all evangelicals admire him and agree with his basic message: "You must be born again!"

As explained in the introduction, an evangelical is defined as anyone who believes in and experiences or practices *conversionism*, *biblicism*, *crucicentrism*, and *activism*. I believe a fifth characteristic of authentic evangelical faith is *respect for the Great Tradition of Christian doctrine*—basic Christian orthodoxy that has been consensually held by Christians (especially Protestants of all types) down through the centuries. As I have made clear elsewhere in this book, much diversity exists among evangelicals; they hold to and practice these five marks in different ways and to different degrees. But these are what make a person or a church evangelical as opposed to "mainline Protestant" or Catholic or something else. (I should add here that I really don't like the term "mainline." I'm just postmodern enough to question whether anything should be baptized "mainline" that automatically makes it the norm for everything else. But sociologists of religion still use it for member churches of the National Council of Churches.)

The Shadow of Emperor Constantine

Unlike affiliates of the Religious Right I do not see any New Testament mandate for Christians to engage in political activism to control the behavior of unbelievers so that it conforms to specifically Christian ethics. Where in the New Testament does Jesus or any apostle even suggest that Christians should get out and try to transform the cultures they live in by taking control of governments to legislate Christian beliefs and values? Did the earliest Christians go around the Roman empire posting the Ten Commandments in public places? Did they run for political office or seek political appointment primarily to take over the culture for Christ? Of course not—and nobody argues that they did. So why do many conservative evangelicals today do such things while claiming to be New Testament Christians? And do all New Testament Christians do such things?

First, many conservative Christians/evangelicals engage in political activism for Christ in the absence of New Testament support because they believe the situation has changed since the first century. Back then Christians could not wield political power, so there was no way to legislate Christian behavior. They didn't even envision a time when Christians would be politically powerful. So the issue didn't come up; the apostles were more concerned with the lives of Christians in the face of heretical movements such as the Gnostics, who promoted libertinism—a kind of theologically justified hedonism.

Then came Constantine in the fourth century—the first Roman emperor to call himself a Christian. Throughout the fourth century Christianity was given more and more favor until near its end another emperor, Theodosius, declared it the state religion. Within a few decades Christians went from hiding in the catacombs and being fed to the lions to being powerful government officials who persecuted other religions! A completely new element entered into Christianity with Constantine and Theodosius. Theologians have called it "Constantinianism"; some call it "Caesaropapism" (Caesar as pope). Whether it manifested in outright theocracy or not, the new element wedded church and state in some manner so that Christians controlled government and culture. This became the norm for over a thousand years.

Then came the Reformation. The medieval synthesis of church, state, and culture was pulled apart by the rise of Protestantism and the ensuing wars of religion. But Constantinianism remained—even among Protestants. In the Swiss city of Geneva Reformer John Calvin attempted to control the city council and the entire ethos of the city by means of powerful persuasion. He was only the city's "chief pastor," but he dominated the city. The city council rarely took action against what he preached and often criminalized behavior he condemned. Under his pastorate in the city heretics were burned at the stake.

The "magisterial Protestants" were those like Luther and Calvin who wanted to keep Constantinianism alive and well in Protestant lands. The "radical Reformers," by contrast, were those like the Anabaptists (e.g., Mennonites) who rejected Constantinianism as inconsistent with the New Testament and called for separation of church and state. Because they were persecuted by Protestants and Catholics alike, they tended to withdraw from public view and practice their faith either in secret or wherever the government would allow it. Their basic premise was that Christians are to live out Jesus' Sermon on the Mount among themselves without in any way attempting to manage history. Managing history is God's business; being obedient to the law of love and following Jesus is the Christian's business.

Both the magisterial Protestants and the radical Protestants believed in transforming culture; they simply had different visions of how best to do it—and so have their followers throughout the centuries. I think theologian H. Richard Niebuhr was mistaken when he contrasted the Anabaptist vision of Christ and culture in the classic book of that title with the Reformed vision (*Christ and Culture* [Harper & Brothers, 1951]). According to Niebuhr and most observers of American religion following him, Reformed Christians (magisterial Protestants) have always held and followed a "Christ transforming culture" model of Christian values and secular society. Anabaptists and other radical Reformers, by contrast, have always held and followed a "Christ against culture" model. This is too static and simplistic. (I hesitate to contradict the great Niebuhr, so I proceed with fear and trembling.) Reformed Christians such as the Puritans of England and New England did, indeed, want to transform culture into the kingdom of God insofar as possible before Christ returns. Their vision of England and New England was based largely on Calvin's Geneva — a Christian commonwealth ruled by Christians and governed according to Christian principles. That vision appears today in some conservative religious groups that seem to want to establish an American theocracy.

The Anabaptist vision, according to Niebuhr, was and is one of withdrawal from society. It is called "sectarian" because its churches have no interest in being culturally influential. They are turned inward on themselves, and for them the kingdom of God only appears now among the sectarian communities; it will permeate all of society and transform culture only by Christ when he returns. In the interim, Niebuhr alleged, Anabaptists are more or less content to let the secular world around them go to hell. (Those are my words and not his, but I think they fairly represent what he wrote.)

In fact, however, Reformed Christians such as the Puritans have always also had a "Christ against culture" model. Not-yet-Christianized culture is depraved and sinful and needs to be invaded by pious Christians who will take over and control it in order to make it more or less a kingdom of God on earth. The extent to which this can be accomplished is a matter of debate among Reformed Christians, but it is wrong to say they are completely devoid of any Christ against culture attitudes. And Anabaptists, though pessimistic about transforming culture into the kingdom of God and shunning any hint of Constantinianism, do care about culture around them. Their way of transforming culture is not direct; it is indirect through creating communities of light that show the world outside the church a better way. They invite the world to come, see, and taste that the Lord is good. By their presence in the midst of the world, they will be salt and light gradually transforming godless culture into something approximating the kingdom of God. They eschew use of political power to do that; it has to be by gentle persuasion and example.

Evangelical Ways of Transforming Culture

Which is the better evangelical way to transform culture? First, let it be said that both ways have always existed side-by-side within the evangelical movement since its beginnings in the Great Awakenings of the early 1700s and early 1800s. Evangelicals such as William Wilberforce of England used government influence to abolish the slave trade. The same happened in America; evangelicals were in the forefront of abolition. Other evangelicals felt it was better to release their slaves and show the world the right way to treat other human beings without attempting to force that on everyone. Some of them established the Underground Railroad and practiced civil disobedience to free slaves and secretly took them to Canada and freedom.

During the pre-Civil War 1800s evangelicals were in the forefronts of various movements to transform society with godly values. Some hoped to turn America into a Christian commonwealth based on Christian principles and values. Others hoped simply to persuade and show by example how to create and live a Christian culture within the church as a "light set on a hill" for the entire world to see.

Near where I live in Waco, Texas, exists a unique intentional Christian community that is based on Anabaptist principles. Homestead Heritage is a church and a farming and crafting community that seeks to live peaceably with everyone and build strong relationships among themselves. They really believe in accountability to each other. They care about the world around them, but instead of forming a political party or a political action committee to change it according to their ideals, they have their own political order and invite people to come and see it. Over forty-five thousand visitors come each year to their festivals, concerts, and craft village/restaurant. They have leadership (elders), but all major decisions are reached only by consensus of the members. Individualism is the enemy, but so is collectivism.

These Christians strive to live in true community guided by the Sermon on the Mount. They view themselves as a city set on a hill to show the world a better way to live. Members go out to help other intentional Christian communities get started; then they come back and invite people to come and see what God is doing among them and how to live an alternative to today's consumer-oriented, individualistic, materialistic society.

Niebuhr's category of "Christ against culture" both fits and does not fit this Christian community and hundreds like it in North America. Yes, they are against the ravages of modern and postmodern culture — especially its ill effects on children. But so are proponents of the "Christ transforming culture" category, such as the old Puritans and the contemporary Religious Right and Christian Reconstructionists, who want the Bible to be the basic law of the United States. The latter groups are just as quick to pit Christian values against modern and postmodern cultural values as any Anabaptist is. The difference is that the Religious Right, most conservative evangelicals, and Christian Reconstructionists believe it is the Christian's duty to change the world using power when persuasion fails. The kingdom of God can be approximated on earth by Christians managing history; "thy will be done on earth as in heaven" is for them a mandate to go into the political realm and triumphalistically take it over and dominate it for Christ and his kingdom.

The Radical Reformation (Anabaptist) View

Anabaptists and similar-minded Christian groups also want to transform the world, but they do not expect to accomplish it triumphalistically by using secular means. They find no warrant in Scripture for Christianizing the social order or even criminalizing behavior Christians regard as sinful. They expect unbelievers to live sinful lives and believe God is their judge. The church's business is to live the kingdom of God within Christian community and thereby be salt and light in the world. They believe that Christians who take on political power over the secular realm in order to Christianize it always end up buying into secular values and compromising the teachings of Jesus about love.

Power corrupts — and that is especially true of political power. The Zealots expected Jesus to overthrow Roman rule over Palestine. But he turned out to be a different kind of Messiah — one who dethrones the distorted powers of this world by suffering. To Anabaptists Jesus Christ is the Lamb of God upon a cross rather than a conquering warrior upon a throne. And Christians should emulate their Master and change the world with love rather than force. Someday Christ will appear as a warrior to defeat his enemies, but in this age, before the final consummation of God's plan, Christians are called to suffer as Christ suffered and not fight for Christian dominance over society.

Conservative evangelicals in the last decades of the twentieth century largely bought into the Christ-transforming culture model. But it contains a large dose of the Christ against culture model. The secular world of culture is viewed as hostile to Christ and Christian values, and Christians are viewed as storm troopers of the kingdom of God, taking over the culture by political force if necessary. But is that the only way to be evangelical and still engage in transforming activism for the kingdom of God? I don't think it is. I have nothing against Christians who run for political office or who hold political offices by appointment. But I don't think that is the only or even the best way to transform the culture. Being salt and light does not require coercion of anyone.

So what is the best way for evangelical Christians to transform the surrounding culture? I believe it is the way practiced by the early Christians of the Roman empire before Constantine and by the radical Reformers of the Reformation. Both groups practiced what Anabaptist theologian John Howard Yoder called voluntary subordination to the powers of this world combined with nonviolent noncooperation with those powers when they require Christians to engage in practices that violate the Word of God and Christian conscience.

Early church father Tertullian wrote to the Roman leaders that "the blood of the martyrs is the seed [of the church]." In other words, the more Christians were persecuted, the more they won converts by exemplifying courage and faithfulness. In effect he was saying, "Go ahead and persecute and kill us; it will just increase our ranks." As the numbers of Christians grew in the Roman cities, their values, lifestyles, and proclamation began to permeate and transform the culture. The same thing happened during the Reformation; the Anabaptists showed European and then North American Christians a better way by example, and eventually that paid off in changes within the culture. What we accept as axiomatic today—separation of church and state and tolerance of religious dissenters—began with them.

So what should evangelical Christians do to transform their culture now? First, they should be the church. Before trying to change society, evangelicals must reform themselves and their congregations and institutions away from individualism, consumerism, and therapeutic Christianity ("your best life now") to radical Christian communities that serve as beacons of faith, hope, and love to the dying world around them. Unfortunately, too many evangelical churches and organizations have taken on the values and behaviors of the secular world while casting aspersions at it. They select certain issues—usually related to sex—and hammer away at them, facing outward toward the culture outside the church while ignoring that there is little difference between the sexual behaviors of committed "Bible Christians" (evangelicals) and non-Christians. In the meantime, they too often adopt secular attitudes and behaviors, such as corporate models of leadership (pastor as CEO) and church growth based on strategies developed by commercial marketers.

It would be so much better for the church and the world if Christians would be content to show a better way to organize community life among themselves. As Yoder never tired of saying, the crucial standard of Christian conduct is obedience and not effectiveness (*The Politics of Jesus* [Eerdmans, 1972, 1992]). Effectiveness in transforming culture may follow obedience, but that's God's business, not ours. Focusing on effectiveness (e.g., how many souls can be saved with a dollar invested in evangelism done a certain way) detracts from obedience in a sinful world.

When obedience to God's way revealed in Jesus Christ is subordinated to effectiveness, the latter always trumps the former, which then ends up falling at least partly by the way.

My suggestion is to let the world of culture outside the church be what it is and will be, leaving it to God to manage history and society. What God has called us to do is obey him, and there is no mandate in Scripture to take over the culture for Christ. The only mandate given to Christians is to follow Jesus Christ in individual and communal life and thereby be "in the world but not of it."

Too often conservative evangelicals have succumbed to being of the world by adopting its political practices of power as domination and control. Christian activism on behalf of the victims of injustice is good and should take the form of prophetic denunciation and annunciation by word and example of a better way. But nothing will speak louder to the world than love and justice practiced within Christian communities. Until and unless that happens, the world of culture can hardly be expected to experience Christian involvement as anything but hypocritical and frightening.

CHAPTER 8

REDISTRIBUTING WEALTH WITHOUT SOCIALISM

During my doctoral studies I served as youth and associate pastor of an inner city church in a large metropolitan area. Our church hosted a "neighborhood pantry," which was supported by several other congregations. People in need came to us for groceries and often I put together their bags of canned and boxed goods. One day a call came from a woman who asked for delivery; she said she had no way to come to the church. So I put two sacks of groceries in my car and went looking for the address. It turned out to be a tiny, unfurnished apartment above an empty store. The stairs were rickety and the lighting poor as I made my way up to the woman's flat. This was as bad a slum as anything I had seen on television.

The woman was in her two-room "apartment" with two small children—both girls dressed in dirty and torn dresses. The only light was a bare bulb hanging from the ceiling. The only furniture was a mattress on the floor. I looked in the kitchen and found its cupboards empty. So was the refrigerator. As I talked with the woman one of her daughters hesitantly approached carrying a moldy orange. She asked if she could eat it. My heart was broken. I left the groceries and promised to bring more.

The next Sunday I told this story to the adult Sunday School class I taught. They offered to take up a love offering to give the woman, but one elderly man—a pillar in the church—protested: "If you give anything to people it makes them dependent." He didn't want money or food taken to the mother and children. "Mr. Jones" was against all forms of welfare and charity, labeling them "socialism." Fortunately the class gave me about $200 to share with the family. A few weeks later I checked on them again and found them living in a clean, little bungalow. The husband had found a job and the woman refused my offer of more food or money. "Mr. Jones" was wrong.

If there is one thing especially associated with being conservative in America, it is belief in a free market economy where government plays a small role in helping people or regulating businesses. Many people simply equate this economic philosophy with capitalism, and many conservative Christians equate capitalism with being Christian and American. Generally speaking, conservatives believe America is great in part because of its free enterprise system; any hint of government interference in the economy to make it fairer for everyone is labeled "socialism." By itself that word is supposed to scare people, and it does scare many conservative Christians.

Why? Well, socialism is another one of those words that has been so abused that it is almost useless. Most people in America simply equate it with "godless communism." It allegedly remains the political and economic system of Cuba, and it has fallen virtually everywhere else. It is inappropriate to stretch the term "socialism" to cover communism because the two are different political and economic systems, though many people think they are the same. In this chapter, I will not advocate socialism (as communism), but I will suggest that evangelical Christianity need not be tied to the free market, free enterprise system and especially not to laissez-faire capitalism (government's "hands off" approach to the economy).

American Christians and Capitalism

Let's begin by defining our terms. In this chapter "free market system," "free enterprise system," and "capitalism" will be used for an economy driven by the desire to gain wealth by investing money in enterprises that will take money away from people by selling them products at a higher price than their actual cost (i.e., the profit motive). Of course, any good economist can punch holes in that definition. Capitalism and the other related terms are much more complex than that. I take it, however, that this is what most people do mean when they talk about the free market system, the free enterprise system, and capitalism.

Since the presidency of Ronald Reagan many people view these systems as synonymous with "Reaganomics" — the view that if enough people gain enough wealth it will automatically benefit everyone in society. A rising tide lifts all boats. Therefore, government's role in the economy is limited; it should regulate as little as possible, interfere in the market economy as little as possible, and *not* redistribute wealth by even indirectly taking money away from the "haves" to give to the "have nots." The have nots can pull themselves up by their own bootstraps by participating in the free enterprise economy as laborers and work their way up the ladder to wealth.

In the era around the turn of the last century a series of books was published based on the fictional life of a young man named Horatio Alger. Horatio was a hard-working, enterprising young man who gained wealth through self-reliance within the capitalistic market economy. The stories were intended to bolster capitalism by inculcating belief that in America anyone can become well off financially simply through hard work. And the free enterprise system is the best economic system known for facilitating that success. People swallowed up the books and the mythos of the self-reliant, hard-working, prosperity-gaining person virtually guaranteed to succeed with capitalism. And they often combined it with their faith so that Horatio Alger became a kind of American saint.

The rise of alternative economic systems such as socialism (public ownership of the means of production) and communism (public ownership of all property) frightened many people in America, and that fright was deepened by Bolshevism in Russia and similar socialistic and communist revolutions elsewhere in the world. The "red scare" was still alive and well when I was a kid in the 1950s. Virtually all evangelical Christians bought into the anticommunist hysteria surrounding the infamous House Select Committee on Unamerican Activities led by Senator Joseph McCarthy. Anticommunist books poured forth into the churches and homes of evangelicals. I remember one of the first books I read (other than children's books) was an anticommunist diatribe by then FBI director J. Edgar Hoover. I swallowed this demagoguery hook, line, and sinker because my parents and relatives did.

That's not to say I approve of communism — especially "godless communism" as it took hold behind the "Iron Curtain" in Eastern Europe and the Soviet Union and then in China and Cuba. But looking back on it now, I see the anticommunism of my youth in a different light. Evangelical Christians began to blend free market capitalism with "God and the American way." Being anticommunist, antisocialist, and procapitalist became part and parcel of being a true, loyal American Christian.

Although the anticommunist hysteria of the ultraconservative conspiracy mongerers of the 1950s has died down, conservative evangelicals still tend to be largely procapitalist and even pro-laissez-faire capitalist. They have been among the harshest critics of Latin American liberation theology, which advocates a transfer of wealth and power to the poor from the 2 to 5 percent of the population who own and control everything in most countries. In the United States conservative evangelicals have often opposed policies such as welfare that seem contrary to the work ethic instilled in them by their Puritan spiritual ancestors.

Problems with American Capitalism and Antiwelfare Attitudes

One example of an influential conservative evangelical who opposes government redistribution of wealth and combines Christianity with capitalism is University of Texas journalism professor and editor of *World* magazine Marvin Olasky. Olasky is one of the architects of what has come to be called "compassionate conservatism." He became an informal advisor of George W. Bush when the latter was governor of Texas. A major network television "news magazine" show called him "Bush's Guru."

Olasky is an intellectual leader among conservative evangelicals; he was a plenary speaker at one annual convention of the National Association of Evangelicals soon after the now fallen Ted Haggard became its president. Through *World* and books such as *Renewing of American Compassion* (Regnery, 1997) he has raised the antiwelfare, antisocialism banner among evangelical Christians and conservatives generally. In his opinion, government should get out of the business of helping people altogether and turn that job over to nonprofit organizations and especially religious ones. He even advocates abolishing the government "safety net" that is supposed to catch and aid the truly indigent and "deserving poor." The main reason is that government-funded welfare programs of all types detract from the compassionate, hands-on help that Christians and others used to give to the needy.

Olasky's proposed alternative to government redistribution of wealth even through welfare programs is for the government to encourage private aid organizations that will help the poor rise above their poverty through job training rather than direct aid. He believes that if the government gets out of the business of redistributing wealth by any means, including job training programs and subsidized day care for the children of poor, working mothers, and offers tax credits for charitable giving, numerous nonprofit organizations will arise to take its place. Redistribution of wealth should be strictly voluntary.

One glaring problem with Olasky's vision is the depravity of human beings. He is theologically a Calvinist and therefore supposedly believes in total depravity. However, he seems hopelessly optimistic about the milk of human kindness or, as Abraham Lincoln called it, the better angels of our human nature. What Olasky seems most opposed to is government entitlement programs—welfare programs that guarantee people who meet certain criteria financial assistance. But if human beings are totally depraved, what would prevent those who organize private, nonprofit welfare programs from limiting their help to people of a certain race, ethnicity, gender, sexual preference, or religion? Government entitlement programs are blind to such differences; anyone who meets the financial criteria for aid must receive it.

Under Olasky's alternative it is conceivable that every nonprofit, private aid organization in a location would exclude people unlike themselves. In some states, for example, every private, nonprofit aid organization might neglect or exclude native Americans. The whole purpose of government entitlement programs is to guarantee that such discrimination does not happen. If it does, those discriminated against have recourse to the courts. That would presumably not be the case in Olasky's America.

Marvin Olasky's influence among conservative evangelicals and on the George W. Bush administration has been tremendous. Just listen attentively to Bush's policy wonks who talk about replacing government welfare with faith-based initiatives funded by the government, which will enable people to stand on their own feet with charitable gifts motivated by tax credits. In Waco, Texas, where I live, such a privately funded, nonprofit organization is Mission Waco, led by Jimmy Dorrell. Mission Waco is not associated in any way with Olasky, but it is the kind of organization Olasky believes could eventually take up the slack left by the demise of government entitlement programs for the poor. Mission Waco runs a number of programs that help the poor and homeless, but even Jimmy Dorrell is doubtful that his or any number of similar organizations can successfully replace government welfare.

Not all conservative evangelicals are opposed to government aid to the poor or other kinds of government-sponsored redistribution of wealth, but most are. That is especially true since the Ronald Reagan presidency, which swept a number of conservative evangelical leaders into powerful positions of influence. The Religious Right consists mostly of conservative evangelicals and opposes redistribution of wealth. An organization associated with the Religious Right publicly opposed tax reform in Alabama that would have made the state's tax system fairer. In that state some working poor people pay higher tax rates than the wealthy. The tax reform proposal was led by an evangelical woman who recently graduated from an evangelical seminary. The state's governor got on board and many people thought the proposal was so blatantly necessary that it would sweep through the legislature. It failed, largely as a result of opposition from the Religious Right.

In Alabama, as in much of the America, conservative evangelicals tend to believe in a flat income tax rate or oppose any income taxes at all (as in Texas). In other words, they believe that every taxpayer should pay, for example, 15 percent to the government in taxes in contrast to the current system in which the wealthy are supposed to pay a higher rate than the poor (but often manage not to because of various tax loopholes). Some conservative evangelicals favor a proposal to replace the national income tax with a national sales tax. These are regressive policies that would hurt the poor.

Evangelical History and Liberal Politics and Economics

I could marshal a large number of Bible passages that urge God's people to care for the poor, but conservative evangelicals argue that these speak of voluntary charitable giving and not government redistribution of wealth. Perhaps so. But if Christians sit in seats of power and influence and have the ability to help the poor with the policies they create, why shouldn't they? Based on Scripture one would think they should. Conservative evangelicals are among the most generous charitable givers in America, but their support of regressive tax systems that either hurt the poor or do nothing for them seems to stand in contradiction to their concern for the poor.

Moreover, in today's America, many people have come to believe that being evangelical necessarily involves strong support for laissez-faire capitalism and opposition to government regulation of business and redistribution of wealth. That's sad because it has not always been the case. In the mid-1800s revivalist B. T. Roberts, founder of the Free Methodist denomination, was the first person to propose an inheritance tax—a visible symbol of government-sponsored redistribution of wealth. Nobody questions Roberts' or the Free Methodists' evangelical credentials. But many of today's evangelicals would think that Roberts was a socialist. In reality, he was a compassionate capitalist who believed government should help the poor by redistributing wealth, based largely on the biblical teachings about the Year of Jubilee (Leviticus 25), in which debts were forgiven.

The Bible, the supreme authority for evangelicals' faith and practice, nowhere mentions capitalism or anything associated with it. How, then, can it be considered the supremely Christian economic system? Many people confuse it with democracy, as if capitalism and democracy are inseparable, but that is a category mistake. Capitalism is an economic system; democracy is a political system. Many socialist countries have democratic governments and many totalitarian governments operate with a capitalist system. Besides, even democracy is not mandated in the Bible; the Bible is strangely silent on these matters.

The closest the Bible comes to speaking about these issues are the many passages in the Old Testament prophets that condemn injustice toward the poor and especially the wealthy getting rich off the labor of the poor. In the New Testament the earliest Christians are said to have held all things in common—a kind of socialistic or communistic system within the Jerusalem church.

Capitalism was virtually unheard of for the first thousand-plus years of Christianity. In fact, throughout the Middle Ages the church forbade lending money at interest. Jewish people were allowed to do it because their religion did not forbid it. The leaders of Christianity believed the Bible taught that usury was a sin. When did things change? During the Renaissance of the fifteenth through the sixteenth centuries, the church began to allow bankers to lend at interest, which gave impetus to entrepreneurship and free enterprise. But not until the eighteenth century did anyone think to give capitalism as a free market economy theological support.

All this raises the question of how anyone can believe capitalism is the one and only truly biblical economic system. It is one thing to believe it is the best economic system in the world, but it is something else entirely to make of it an idol by attaching it to Christianity in the way many conservative Christians do. My point is not to condemn capitalism; I happen to believe some modified form of democratic capitalism works best, given human depravity (and thus the need for a motive to work and invest). A purely socialistic or communistic system in which there exists little or no incentive to work hard to earn money or to invest to start a business to employ people simply does not function well. Most countries that have tried it have eventually turned back to capitalism in some form.

Many evangelicals believe that capitalism unchecked by strong government regulation of businesses to prevent monopolies and other abuses tends toward injustice. In that they agree with the Catholic bishops around the world, including the United States Catholic Bishops Conference. We also believe that one of government's functions should be to redistribute wealth to balance the inequities that tend to appear in any capitalist system. How can it be just for CEOs of corporations to earn millions and gather billions of dollars while children in their communities go to bed hungry at night? The gap between the rich and the poor tends to widen in any unregulated and unchecked capitalist system.

In my own lifetime some evangelical Christian leaders have advocated redistribution of wealth — both voluntary through charity and government-sponsored through highly graduated income taxes, combined with entitlement programs to help the neediest citizens (especially children). When I was a young man one of the most powerful and influential members of the U.S. Congress was Senator Mark Hatfield of Oregon, who was also openly and unapologetically evangelical. Although he was a Republican, he advocated government aid to the poor and was generally considered a moderate if not a liberal.

There were other moderate and liberal Republicans in the 1960s and early 1970s, including an evangelical politician from Illinois who ran for president as an Independent and won about 7 percent of the popular vote. His name was John Anderson, a member of the Evangelical Free Church of America — a leading evangelical Christian denomination. (I cast my presidential vote for him in 1980!) Hatfield and Anderson were not alone; not long ago many evangelicals believed government should play a leading role in redistributing wealth.

Redistributing Wealth without Socialism Using Reason and Scripture

How should wealth be redistributed without socialism? By means of a highly graduated income tax combined with government entitlement programs focused on job training and placement, free day care for children of the working poor, and universal health coverage for every American. These are not unreasonable or unchristian policies; they accord well with Scripture's overt concern for the poor and oppressed. The idea that taxes are a form of government theft comes from the philosophy of secular thinkers like Robert Nozick of Harvard University. Unfortunately, too many conservative evangelical Christians have bought into them.

One has to wonder what role an implicit social Darwinism plays in the antigovernment welfare and antitax movements in the U.S. and even among Christians. Nozick seems to have been infected with that philosophy that says that the poor are the weaker of the human species and nature's basic law is survival of the fittest, so we should not help the poor survive; it corrupts the gene pool. Few people actually say such things, but lying in the deep background of too much conservative thinking about issues like welfare and poverty is this social form of Darwin's evolutionary theories. The irony should not escape us. Many conservative Christians oppose biological evolution while implicitly and unconsciously promoting a form of social Darwinism.

What does the Bible say about the poor and the rich? There's a wealth of material there, and much of it is overlooked especially in conservative churches. Let's just take three examples — two from the Old Testament and one from the New Testament. Isaiah 3:14 condemns the rich of Israel who have "devoured the vineyard" so that the "spoil of the poor" is in their houses. God asks them in 3:15: "What do you mean by crushing my people, by grinding the face of the poor?" This passage refers to the lack of compassion toward the poor and especially their exploitation by the rich, who were supposed to leave some of the crops for the poor. Instead, they took everything and hoarded it for themselves and their families. This clearly refers to oppression of the poor; blame for their misery is placed at the feet of the rich rather than on laziness in the poor or their lack of a work ethic.

Ezekiel 22:12 hints at how the rich oppress the poor: "you ... take bribes to shed blood; you take interest and increase and make gain of your neighbors by extortion; and you have forgotten me, says the Lord God." This is one biblical passage on which the church rested its case against loaning money at interest for about a thousand years. Many other Old Testament passages talk about the oppression of the poor by the rich and call for justice for the poor.

James 5:1–6 is the Bible's harshest diatribe against the rich and their oppression of the poor:

> Come now, you rich, weep and howl for the miseries that are coming upon you. Your riches have rotted and your garments are moth-eaten. Your gold and silver have rusted, and their rust will be evidence against you and will eat your flesh like fire. You have laid up treasure for the last days. Behold, the wages of the laborers who mowed your fields, which you kept back by fraud, cry out; and the cries of the harvesters have reached the ears of the Lord of hosts. You have lived on the earth in luxury and in pleasure; you have fattened your hearts in a day of slaughter. You have condemned, you have killed the righteous man; he does not resist you.

Of course, someone might claim that this refers only to those few rich who have failed to pay their laborers, but I doubt it. The condemnation is of all hoarding of goods in a time and place where there are poor people. Too often conservative churches have glossed over this and other passages about wealth and poverty in the Bible and interpreted them so that they do not threaten the vested interests of the wealthy. Overall, however, not only this passage but the entire Bible cries out for justice for the poor and hurls invectives at the rich.

Not only does the Bible nowhere endorse capitalism, but it contains condemnations of capitalism's excesses as well—especially a growing gap between the rich and the poor. The rich have a responsibility for the poor. They are not to exploit them or oppress them. They are to leave them some of their crops. They are not to loan them money at interest. It is difficult to square these biblical teachings about wealth and poverty with many conservative evangelical Christians' uncritical embrace of laissez-faire capitalism and opposition to redistribution of wealth. Nowhere does the Bible command absolute economic equality, and it does command work. But does "work" include investing money? That's debatable. Many rich people gain wealth without actually working. Redistributing wealth is implied in the Bible's injunctions to the rich and powerful (see 1 Timothy 6:17–19), though not at the expense of work and productivity. The so-called "welfare state" is not obviously or overtly biblical, but neither is the state that neglects the poor.

An inevitable question at this point is whether the Bible's commands to care for the poor aim only at voluntary charity. In other words, are Christians required to favor and work toward public policies that encourage redistribution of wealth on behalf of the poor? Not explicitly. And as argued in the previous chapter, Christians are not called to take over society to establish morality or justice using government power.

So what should a Christian who believes in justice for the poor, including redistribution of wealth, do beyond charitable giving to the poor? One important consideration here is whether there are also secular reasons to argue for and attempt to implement government policies that encourage redistribution of wealth. In other words, a Christian who comes to believe government ought to redistribute wealth to lessen the gap between the rich and the poor might use a secular argument that puts feet to his or her spiritual motives. That's not the same as taking over the culture for Christ; it means combining a spiritual motive with a secular argument in order to arrive at just public policies.

John Rawls was a secular philosopher at Harvard University; he taught there at about the same time as Robert Nozick. The two held nearly opposite views of the rights of the poor and the obligations of the rich. Nozick believed in small government that interferes as little as possible in the economy. Rawls believed in limited but active government and developed a theory of justice as fairness. His book *A Theory of Justice* (Belknap, 2005) has become a classic of modern social ethics and is widely read and studied in both secular and religious colleges and universities. Rawls argued that the right policy is one that all reasonable people would agree on if they did not know their own powers and vested interests.

Rawls asked readers to imagine an original situation (like a convention of all people) in which a "veil of ignorance" hides from people their own social status and powers. They have no idea what their advantages and disadvantages will be when the veil of ignorance is lifted. He argued that whatever social policies, such as equitable taxation, they would agree on under the veil of ignorance would be fair. And he argued that under the veil of ignorance they would opt for a system in which increases in wealth for some people would automatically enhance the economic situation of those lower on the economic ladder. The principle is "maximizing the minimum."

One way to do that is a highly graduated income tax combined with redistribution of wealth to the poor through education, job training, direct aid to children, subsidized day care for children of poor working mothers and fathers, and other forms of welfare. The aim would be to maximize poor people's opportunities to participate in the economy. One might argue that Rawls' principle would also require guaranteed work with a living wage for everyone and universal entitlement to health care. These social policies are often labeled "socialism" by conservatives, but that should not scare anyone. It's just a word. In fact, these are not socialistic policies; they are simply adjustments to capitalism to ameliorate its tendency to widen the gap between the rich and the poor.

Christianity and the Poor

There seem to be plenty of reasons, both biblical and secular, to believe in and promote the welfare of the poor in a capitalist society. Too many conservative evangelicals pay lip service to it while their support for laissez-faire capitalism and opposition to welfare in any form tend to belie that. No biblical or rational conflict confronts the evangelical Christian who wants to advocate for the poor, including government-sponsored redistribution of wealth, in spite of all the fussing and fuming of some conservative evangelicals who consider such policies socialistic.

Of course, Marvin Olasky is correct about one thing. Compassion for the poor must go beyond advocating government policies on their behalf. It must include hands-on work among and with the poor; it should also include identification with them. Although Olasky doesn't say it, I think compassion requires the church to become a church of the poor. By that I mean that a biblical church ought never to flee the urban centers of America in order to attract the powerful and wealthy in the suburbs. It's certainly okay to plant new churches wherever people live, but the flight of evangelical churches from city centers to affluent suburbs is a travesty.

Some evangelical churches, such as the one my wife and I attend, have opted to stay in the inner city and even embark on building campaigns to make their buildings more inviting and accessible to the neighbors. They have adjusted their worship services to fit the ethnic and linguistic complexions of their neighborhoods. They have urged their congregants to move into those neighborhoods around the church in what is called "intentional neighboring" in order to identify with the poor, the immigrants, the indigent, and the homeless and to be salt and light among them.

This stands in stark contrast to too many evangelical churches and mission organizations that aim their ministries primarily at the rich and powerful—even in other countries. Where would Jesus go? To the rich and powerful? Yes. But also to the poor and oppressed. Evangelicals who have hearts for the poor and oppressed, the outcasts and downtrodden of society, have nothing for which to apologize. They are every bit as evangelical as those who favor unregulated and unlimited capitalism—and perhaps more so. Redistribution of wealth is biblical; an ever-widening gap between the rich and the poor is not. A person can be more evangelical by being less conservative when it comes to economics.

CHAPTER 9

RELATIVIZING WITHOUT REJECTING THEOLOGY

When I first thought about becoming a theologian, I asked my college theology professor to recommend a volume that would show me a model of evangelical theological thinking. He suggested a hefty tome on the end times written by a leading conservative evangelical scholar who taught at a dispensational seminary. "Dispensational" refers to the common evangelical system of belief about the future: Jesus Christ will return to earth to "rapture" Christians before the Great Tribulation period, after which he will return again in judgment to begin his millennial reign on earth. I tried to read the book but found it beyond my capacity to understand. The author seemed to know much more than the Bible says about the future. His approach to biblical interpretation and theology seemed speculative, overly literal, and dogmatic. Eventually I quit reading and decided perhaps I should never be a theologian if this book was any indication of what that means. So far as I could tell, the author believed any good Christian would agree with him about the details of the end times.

A hallmark of conservative theologians is a tendency to believe that the Bible is a not-yet-systematized collection of propositions about God waiting to be organized into a system of theology.

Another hallmark is their tendency to downplay or deny a gap between the Bible itself as God's Word and their own interpretations of it. Many of these conservative theologians are evangelicals and their names come readily to mind whenever "evangelical theology" is mentioned. Look on the shelves marked "theology" in most any Christian bookstore (and marked "Christianity" in many secular bookstores) and you'll find their books. Apparently this kind of highly systematized treatment of Christian doctrines is what many evangelicals want. Others, especially postmodern and postconservative evangelicals, find these usually massive tomes of dogmatics tedious and even misguided in their pretense of setting forth the "clear teachings" of the Bible acknowledging that much of the systematized discussion of theology is a result of the author's own reading of the biblical texts.

What Theology Is or Should Be

Let's begin by talking about "theology." It's an ambiguous word; people use it in different ways. Sometimes it simply means the beliefs of a particular denomination or theologian. For example, people will refer to "Karl Barth's theology." (Barth was one of the twentieth century's most influential Protestant theologians.) Or "Roger Olson's theology." (Probably not often mentioned, but in this case it would refer to my beliefs as stated in *The Mosaic of Christian Belief* [InterVarsity Press, 2002]).

Another use of "theology" is to label any thinking about God. In fact, that's what the term actually means: "God thinking" (a combination of the Greek words for "God" and "thought"). In this case someone might say "Karl Barth's theology" or "Roger Olson's theology" (I like to mention myself in the same sentence as Karl Barth!) and mean our distinctive ways of thinking about God. For example, Barth's style of thinking about God was always to begin with Jesus Christ as our best clue to the nature and character of God. Another theologian might begin with the Bible as a divinely inspired repository of equally authoritative propositions about God. That describes the method of theology used by the all-important nineteenth-century theologian Charles Hodge, whose influence still lingers over most conservative evangelical theologizing. Yet another theologian might begin with human experience. That tends to be the way liberal theologians "do theology."

My preferred way of theologizing is to follow the so-called "Wesleyan Quadrilateral." The label was coined by Wesley scholar Albert Outler in the 1960s, but it aptly describes the way John Wesley, the founder of the Methodist tradition, practiced theology. The quadrilateral posits four authoritative sources and norms for Christian theologizing: Scripture, tradition, reason, and experience. (These form the sides of the quadrilateral with truth as we know it in the middle.) Theologians who use this method argue whether the quadrilateral is an equilateral or whether Scripture trumps the other three sources and norms. As an evangelical, I use the quadrilateral not as an equilateral. For me Scripture (including Jesus Christ as the interpretive center) trumps tradition, reason, and experience. To be more precise about how I do theology, I recognize Scripture and tradition as the two sources and norms of theology (with Scripture primary and the Great Tradition of Christian belief secondary) and reason and experience as interpretive tools to help us sort out and understand Scripture and tradition.

My impression (and I know I'm not alone) is that conservative theologians tend to place tradition on the same plane of authority as Scripture without admitting it. Roman Catholic theologians admit it; tradition is in some sense equal with Scripture. (Well, there's been a lot of discussion about that in Catholic theology since Vatican II in the 1960s.) But Protestants have always insisted on *sola scriptura*, which means that Scripture trumps tradition whenever there's a conflict. It doesn't mean tradition is bad or something to be ignored or discarded. That's impossible; we all think along with some tradition as we read and interpret the Bible. What it means is that everything in Christian tradition is open to question in the light of Scripture and Jesus Christ is the touchstone for interpreting Scripture. (Martin Luther said the Bible is the cradle that brings us the Christ.)

Theology, Systems, and Tradition

My concern is that too many conservative evangelical theologians, pastors, teachers, and laypeople inadvertently elevate some tradition as the authoritative interpretive lens through which Scripture is read and understood. But that is, in effect, to place tradition on the same plane as Scripture. If the church is to be constantly renewed and reformed, tradition has to take a back seat to the inscripturated Word of God. But the conservative habit of mind is to jump to the defense of "what we've always believed" or "the received evangelical tradition" when some new idea (such as open theism) arises. In my opinion, based on twenty-five years of teaching theology within evangelicalism, conservative theology defends the status quo. It tends to absolutize some system of doctrine and make it unchangeable except in how it is expressed to each new generation.

Conservative evangelical theologians have tended to do this with the systematic theology of Charles Hodge, the great patriarch of the Old Princeton School of Theology in the 1800s. Hodge wrote a three-volume *Systematic Theology*, which was supposedly nothing more or less than a scientific mining of truths out of Scripture and placing them in an orderly, logical system of truth. Hodge compared theology to science. Just as the natural sciences look at the material world of nature and draw facts from a careful, objective investigation of it, so theology looks objectively into Scripture and draws facts out of it and expresses them in a system of doctrines. Most conservative evangelical theologians in the past century have tended to use this "scientific method" even if they did not agree entirely with all of Hodge's conclusions.

Models of Evangelical Theology

Is this pattern the only way of doing evangelical theology, and is there even such a thing as a final product of theological discovery? I notice two distinct attitudes among evangelical theologians (and the pastors and laypeople they influence). One is the fortress model of theology. People who follow this pattern believe that all-important questions about God have been answered and they are suspicious of new discoveries or alterations in what they consider the received evangelical tradition of doctrine. So what does theology do now? For conservatives, who largely follow the fortress model, theology's contemporary tasks are to defend the received tradition (e.g., Hodge's system of doctrines) and restate it in modern language so that contemporary people can understand and receive it.

The other approach among evangelicals is what I call the pilgrimage model. These theologians are evangelical because they recognize Scripture as the divinely inspired, authoritative Word of God. Often, however, they do not regard it as a not-yet-systematized collection of propositional truths to be mined and then systematized. They might view the Bible instead as a drama. Interpreting it is more an art than a science, and one has to be an actor in the drama really to understand the Bible.

The Bible, in other words, is a fantastic story of God's interactions with humans. It begins with creation, continues with corruption, and is followed by correction (covenant, Christ, and church) and consummation. It has characters and plot and is to be read as a realistic story. Not fiction, but truth expressed in literature, not just facts. In this style of doing evangelical theology (often called "narrative theology"), stories that cannot be reduced to information bring transformation to people. Human lives are shaped more by stories than by systems of facts. God has given us a story, draws us into it, and leaves it up to us to continue the unfinished drama. New Testament scholar and Church of England bishop N. T. Wright compares the Bible and tradition to an unfinished play and we Christians are the actors. We have four acts of the play (Scripture and faithful tradition) and are called to faithful improvisation of the rest of the play.

This second model of doing theology implies a theological pilgrimage. Theologians are like explorers or pilgrims on a journey. Switching metaphors, Scripture and tradition are our map and our guide. If the guide (tradition) seems to be leading us away from the itinerary on the map, we have a right to question him and even correct him. For the most part, he is trustworthy. But he's not infallible. Only the map is infallible. But even the map is complicated and needs careful study and interpretation. Scripture is like a map without a legend (the little box on most maps that tells what symbols mean). It's up to us to watch it carefully as we follow our guide and keep looking at the territory around us to be sure the guide is really following the map and not leading us astray.

This model of doing evangelical theology relativizes theology without rejecting it. This means that theology is "second order" language of the Christian and the church. It is not our primary language. That's God's speech to us and our response in worship and devotion. But just because theology is second order does not mean it is unimportant. We are called to use our God-given minds to interpret the clues embedded in God's speech to us (through the drama and the map) and continue the play faithfully or continue the journey critically and carefully.

The point is that for this second model of doing evangelical theology there is no such thing as a final system of theology that is not open to correction. All theologies (using here the first sense of theology mentioned above) are fallible and incomplete because they are truly man-made and not handed down from God. Only Scripture is that. And no system of theology can take the place of Scripture because Scripture is not a not-yet-systematized collection of propositions. Tradition, including even the greatest theological expressions in creeds, confessions of faith, and systems of doctrine, is not our highest authority. Scripture trumps tradition. In any discernment of truth situation tradition gets a vote but never a veto.

Furthermore, the collective spiritual experience of God's people is a necessary tool for refocusing our attention on Scripture. Experience shaped, but not determined, by history and culture can rightly cause the Christian community to interrogate tradition and study Scripture with fresh eyes, finding lost or neglected elements of the light. In this sense, God always has new light to break forth from his Word. It's not that new revelations occur; it's that new situations arise in our experience that demand a fresh and faithful look at Scripture.

Examples of "Pilgrimage Theology"

As an example of fresh and faithful interpretation of Scripture in the light of experience, let's start with the Reformation. Conservative evangelicals love to extol the courage of Martin Luther and other Reformers who looked at the Bible with fresh eyes and went against a thousand years of tradition because Scripture demanded it. In other words, Luther noticed that the church of his day was not faithfully extending the unfinished drama of God's Word into the present and toward the future. The director (the pope) and the actors (clergy and theologians) were getting away from the story line. Luther dared to say a firm "no" to tradition and call Christians back to the Bible. He began a new troupe of actors to stand on the stage and faithfully improvise the extension of the drama in his time and place. The point is that Luther's experiences (and those of others in his community) caused him to take a new look at the old drama (Scripture) and reconsider everything he had been told to believe and do by the play's director. He found he was out of step with the play as it was being conducted by the actors guided by the director.

What experiences led Luther to reconsider the doctrines and practices of the church of his time? One was his trip to Rome for the Augustinian order of monks. There he saw with his own eyes how corrupt and abusive the church had become. Another experience was studying the book of Romans in his university tower room—his so-called "Tower Experience"—in which he felt led by the Spirit of God to focus on certain neglected and misinterpreted passages. Another experience was his encounter with poor people who were purchasing indulgences from Rome's indulgence peddlers, who promised them time out of purgatory if they paid money to help build St. Peter's Basilica in Rome. This experience forced Luther to look into Scripture with fresh but still faithful eyes and reinterpret it.

As I said, Luther is a hero to most conservative evangelical theologians. But the ironic tragedy is that too often they now fill the role of those inquisitors who demanded that Luther recant his newly discovered truths and stop improvising the unfinished drama in his new way. Out of the Reformation came a principle for all Protestants always to follow: *reformata et semper reformanda* — reformed and always reforming. In other words, Christians are always to remain open to changes in doctrine and practice insofar as they are required by Scripture.

I often wonder what would happen to Luther if he arrived today at many conservative evangelical institutions and churches and nailed a new ninety-five theses to their doors. I fear that he would be driven away or at least criticized for breaking with the received evangelical tradition. But how can the church be reformed and always reforming if it doesn't allow for new Luthers with their desire and ability to make the Word fresh by discovering the new light breaking forth from it?

You see, we nonconservative evangelicals do not elevate experience to a level equal with Scripture. But we recognize that just as Luther's experiences forced his nose down deeper into Scripture and led him to break with the tradition of his day, so contemporary theologians must be accorded the freedom to question traditional dogmas in the light of their experiences, driving them to faithfully reconsider what the Bible says and means and implies for the ongoing improvisation of the drama.

Let's follow the example of Luther with another illustration of how experience can spark reconsideration of traditional interpretations of Scripture. Just as most conservative evangelicals would agree that Luther was justified in breaking from and correcting tradition in his day, so they would agree that in the 1800s Christian abolitionists were right to contradict the centuries of biblical and theological justification of slavery and demand that all the slaves be set free. William Wilberforce was an evangelical member of the British parliament who experienced the horrors of the slave trade. He met a former slave trader named John Newton, the author of the hymn "Amazing Grace," and heard from him how the slaves were treated by their captors. He went to some slave-transporting ships and saw firsthand the tortures that slaves endured on the way from Africa to be sold to Europeans and Americans.

These experiences impelled him to read Scripture with fresh eyes and there he found something more than the traditional justification of slavery, namely, that the Bible nowhere condemns it or orders Christians to free their slaves. He found instead that God created all men and women in his image and likeness, that Christ died for all people, and that Christian masters of slaves were asked to treat their slaves as their brothers (the book of Philemon). Wilberforce and other Christian abolitionists drew on biblical principles to argue that the drama of the Bible is not finished. God has more light to break forth from his Word. Freeing the slaves did not contradict the Bible and it did fulfill some implicit director's notes that had been ignored.

Now conservative evangelicals look back at Luther and Wilberforce and think that such reforming work that goes against tradition is finished. But why should we think that? Have we then arrived at a full and final system of belief and practice of the Christian life that needs no further correction? How can that be? Isn't such an attitude toward doctrines, systems of theology, and church practices a form of idolatry? What would Luther say? What would Wilberforce say? We could add in Martin Luther King and the Christian feminists, such as those in the Christians for Biblical Equality organization. What would and do they say? Conservative evangelical theologians and administrators of organizations, schools, and publishing houses too often betray the reforming spirit of Luther by hardening the categories so that something labeled "traditional" cannot be questioned or changed. Change is risky, but so is life. Theology should be a risk also. Otherwise it is boring and useless.

Theology and Experience

Experience is presently forcing some evangelicals to question traditional evangelical beliefs and habits. I'm not placing them on the same level as Luther or even Wilberforce. But I am arguing that they should not be shut down or off just because what they are saying is troubling in that it contradicts evangelical tradition. Conservative evangelical theologians and leaders often react too quickly and too negatively to proposed changes in traditional doctrines and biblical interpretations.

One contemporary example of changes taking place in the ongoing improvisation of the unfinished drama of Scripture and Christian tradition is a new view of God's omniscience called "open theism." It is also sometimes known as "the openness of God" or simply "open God view." I am privileged to know some of the leaders of this proposed new interpretation of God's omniscience; some of them have been my friends for years. I also regard some of their leading evangelical critics as friends. So I have been in the middle of the debate.

Open theists (and some who don't use that label for themselves) argue that the traditional theological idea of God's relationship to time is mistaken if not simply illogical and unbiblical and that traditional belief about God's knowledge of the future is theologically incorrect. Spurred by experiences such as encounters with evil and tragedy, these postconservative evangelicals dare to propose that God is not timeless but temporal and that God does not know the future exhaustively and infallibly. Well, actually, that description comes more from their critics than from the open theists themselves! Conservative evangelical critics of open theism have at times reacted with near hysteria to its popularity among younger evangelicals through the influence of open theists such as Gregory Boyd, Clark Pinnock, and John Sanders. One could throw in nonevangelicals such as British physicist and theologian John Polkinghorne and German theologian Jürgen Moltmann (I have personally confirmed with both of them that they share the open theistic view of the future and of God's knowledge).

So what is the open theists' account of their proposed alterations in traditional doctrine? They insist that it is not so much an alteration in the doctrine of God as in the traditional notion of the future. Based on the idea that God is "above" or "outside" of time, which they consider speculative rather than biblical, people assume that the future is already actual in some sense — at least to God. But the Bible portrays God as in time with us; the biblical God is part of the drama. He's the author *and* main actor. He interacts with people and allows them to affect him; their prayers change his plans. A timeless, nontemporal God could not do this. He could not be changed in any way by what is happening in time.

This idea of God's voluntary entrance into time with us is not as controversial among conservative evangelicals as the open theists' next step. They say that since the future partly consists of contingent, potential, not-yet-settled events, nobody can know it exhaustively or infallibly. Events that are not yet determined, such as free moral decisions and actions of human beings, simply cannot yet be known because they don't exist. Arguing that God's omniscience must include such events is like arguing that God's omniscience must include knowing the DNA of unicorns. There's nothing to know. Open theists all agree that God knows everything that is possible as possible; he knows all possibilities. And he knows the future — that part of it that is already determined, such as his own unalterable plans and decrees. Open theists then support these views of the future and God's omniscience with Scripture and reason, knowing they go against most of Christian tradition. But, like Luther, they are willing to take the risk of siding with what they believe Scripture and reason say against tradition. (At his trial before the emperor Luther said that he could not recant his views about salvation because it would be to go against Scripture and reason.)

The conservative evangelical reaction to open theism was immediately to pounce on it as clearly wrong. Why? Because we all know that God is omniscient and cannot be limited in his knowledge. (Most of the critics are Calvinists who also believe

God determines the future and therefore, of course, knows it. Open theists are not Calvinists; they believe God delegates some power to decide the future to human beings.) But why do "we all know" that God's omniscience must include his ability to know the future exhaustively and infallibly? Well, because that's the traditional view; it was settled long ago. Of course, some conservative evangelicals have tried to debate open theism using Scripture and not tradition, but their interpretations of Scripture are traditional and they don't seem willing to reconsider them.

What is at stake in this controversy? Open theists say "not much." All evangelical Christians pray as if God does not know the future exhaustively and infallibly (or that the future is not yet fully actual and therefore can be moved one way or another). What really changes if we say God does not know the future completely because much of it is not yet there to know? Some people claim to take comfort in the idea that they "know who holds tomorrow." But open theists believe God is omniresourceful and can handle whatever happens in the future; they believe exactly the same about God's power as conservatives. Comfort really lies in knowing that God is in charge and can work powerfully in response to prayer to take care of his people. His knowing every detail of the future already does not afford any real comfort. Conservative theologians claim that what is at stake is God's ability to steer the future according to his plan. But why? If God is all powerful and omniresourceful, he can steer the future by his power and resourcefulness whichever direction it may begin to take.

What really seems to be at stake in this debate is tradition. Conservatives are simply nervous about any significant changes in traditional evangelical beliefs. They think that if this change is allowed, who knows what will be changed next? Is everything up for grabs? Doesn't theology ever simply settle something and beyond that point no alteration is allowed? If that's not the case, then aren't we stuck in the swamp of relativism? Isn't God's absolute foreknowledge part of the firm foundation beneath our evangelical feet?

One can certainly sympathize with this conservative concern. Like them I revere the Great Tradition of Christian teaching, including that God knows the future exhaustively and infallibly. But unlike them, I have to admit that *if* it turns out the open theists are supported by a fresh and faithful interpretation of the Bible and reason, open theism is at least an evangelical option and perhaps a doctrine we must embrace. So far I am not convinced that we must embrace open theism; the case for it is still being made and there are problems for open theists to resolve.

Open Theology

This is why I'm not conservative theologically. Today "conservative" in theology does not simply mean "acknowledging the Bible as God's authoritative Word," as one pastor told me. No, today conservative means defending the "faith once and for all delivered" (or discovered) against every new idea that seems to go against it. I can't see how evangelicals can be conservative in that sense. In my opinion, one can be more evangelical by being open to new ideas arising from fresh and faithful reading of the Bible than by sticking stubbornly to old ones. That's because part of being evangelical is commitment to the Bible as God's Word possibly overruling tradition.

Of course, advocates of nontraditional views such as open theism must also remain open to correction in light of God's Word, and they should take the Great Tradition of Christian belief seriously as a secondary norm and should break with it only reluctantly. However, the great heroes of most evangelical traditions were rebels in their own times. Wesleyan evangelicals put John Wesley on a pedestal because he went against the religious establishment of his own time and dared to question the authority of its traditions. For example, he argued from the Bible and experience that Christians can experience a kind of perfection in this life before the resurrection. Until Wesley virtually all Protestants considered that a Catholic idea ("the saints"). Wesley reinterpreted the Bible, found the idea there, and dared to teach it, knowing that it contradicted traditional interpretations of Scripture among other evangelicals of his day, such as George Whitefield, his Calvinist fellow evangelist.

Calvinists in the Reformed tradition (which make up the majority of conservative evangelical theologians) revere John Calvin, the reformer of Geneva in the sixteenth century. But Calvin was a rebel against the Catholic Church and had to flee France because of his nontraditional views. Baptists look back with pride to John Smyth, Thomas Helwys (the first Baptists), and Roger Williams (the man who brought the Baptist faith to America). But all of them were rebels against the Church of England and the Congregationalists out of whose ranks they came. They dared to refuse baptism to infants and baptized only adult believers. That was a major shift away from universal Christian tradition when it began in the 1500s among the Anabaptists.

My point is that evangelical heroes of the past were not very conservative. All of them were heroes precisely because they dared to break away from tradition on the basis of fresh and faithful readings of Scripture usually spurred by experience. But they were not relativists or destroyers of all doctrine. Nor did any of them toss aside all of Christian tradition but kept and valued parts of it that were biblical. Somehow today, it seems, conservative evangelicals are acting like those traditionalists who opposed their own heroes and sometimes persecuted them! I don't say that of all conservatives, but it is a noticeable and common habit of the conservative evangelical theological mind.

So what's the answer? How can one be evangelical but not theologically conservative? The answer is by holding fast to the experience of being transformed by the power of the Holy Spirit bringing a person into union with Jesus Christ called conversion and by standing firmly and unwaveringly on the authority of the Bible over tradition. Finally, yes, by respecting the Great Tradition of Christian doctrine even as one has to question parts of it from time to time and be willing to alter it when necessary. None of this implies relativism; by no means am I suggesting that changes in traditional beliefs should be based on culture or philosophy or even experience. Experience serves only as the catalyst for looking freshly into the Bible to see if traditional interpretations are correct. The final word on that is Scripture itself.

CHAPTER 10

UPDATING WITHOUT TRIVIALIZING WORSHIP

A popular church in a southern California city attracts hundreds, if not thousands, of attendees at worship services every Sunday morning. I visited there two Sunday mornings while commuting to teach on weekends at a nearby seminary. The traditional service of worship was rather formal and stiff; some would say lifeless. Few people under fifty attended. The pastor introduced some elements of liturgy into the otherwise Baptist worship style. The people at the traditional service were by and large educated, upper middle class, professional or business people. The sermons were calm and occasionally leaned a little to the "left" (liberal) of the denomination's theological style.

Another worship service went on at the same time as the traditional one. The pastor went from the sanctuary to the church's gymnasium to preach a narrative-style sermon to this younger and more "hip" crowd of contemporary worshipers. The gym was crowded with college kids and twenty-somethings. The atmosphere was relaxed and, some would say, irreverent. Two young men imitated "Hans and Franz" of the well-known *Saturday Night Live* skit series. The congregation (or audience) observed and laughed while drinking sodas or bottled water. There was no hint of liturgy and the sermon leaned more to the "right" (conservative) for this crowd.

What's going on with this fairly common scenario in contemporary evangelical churches?

One of the great ironies of contemporary evangelicalism in America is that theologically conservative churches are often the first ones to update worship while more liberal churches tend to hold onto traditional liturgies or even return to older forms of worship. This is one reason the labels "conservative" and "liberal" (or "progressive") get distorted; people assume they describe churches' worship styles. They picture a conservative church as one with traditional worship and reluctance to try out new styles of worship, such as having a worship "band" and singing contemporary Christian music. Then they picture a liberal church as one where people like to sing contemporary "praise and worship" choruses to the beat of drums and bass guitars and perhaps dance a little (or a lot).

For years I have had to correct these notions among my theology students. Until they learn what "conservative" and "liberal" really mean in theological terms (which is how these labels are usually assigned to churches by scholars), they think such labels refer to old-fashioned worship and to experimental, up-to-date worship that appeals to youth.

Unity in Evangelical Worship

There is no one "evangelical" style of worship. In this area evangelicals are probably as diverse as any other religious community in America. Once again, it may be helpful for readers who have skipped right to this chapter to review briefly what makes a person, church, or organization "evangelical." (This is laid out in more detail in the introduction.)

First, evangelicals have a certain attitude toward the Bible, called *biblicism*. Second, evangelicals believe that an experience called conversion is the necessary gateway to salvation and authentic Christian living. This is called *conversionism* and results in what many evangelicals call a "personal relationship with Jesus Christ." Third, evangelical devotion is cross-centered (i.e., *cruci-*

centrism); the atoning death of Jesus Christ is the only basis for salvation (rightness with God) and the center of all preaching and living. Fourth, evangelicals are activists (*activism*) for evangelism and social transformation. They do not all agree on how to do those things, but they agree that Christians are called by God to be his partners in redeeming the world by spreading the gospel and helping the poor and oppressed.

Fifth and final, evangelicals all hold the Great Tradition of Christian doctrine in high respect. Doctrine matters to evangelicals, more to some than others. But to be evangelical means to confess truth about God drawn from the Bible (*sola scriptura*) and interpreted through the lens of the church fathers and the Reformers. This I call *respect for right doctrine*. Scripture stands above traditional doctrines as their judge. Whatever conflicts with Scripture cannot be held as true doctrine. As we saw in the previous chapter, reform of doctrine in the light of Scripture is a good thing, so long as it does not involve a wholesale discarding of the Christian tradition as false (which is usually a mark of a cult).

What, then, are the marks of evangelical worship? Are there any common characteristics if not necessary ones? Are there family resemblances of worship among evangelicals? Except for the five characteristics of authentic evangelical life discussed above, there are none. All evangelicals exalt the crucifixion of Christ in worship. They may not display a cross, but they will probably sing some songs about Jesus' death for our sins and urge people to embrace the atoning death of Christ by repentance and faith in him. All evangelicals will use the Bible in worship and treat it as God's inspired, written Word. All evangelicals will call people to personal faith in Christ even if they have been baptized as infants. All will engage in some form of evangelism and social action even if only by participating in offerings for missions and charitable works. Finally, they all will teach the basic doctrines of Christianity: the deity of Jesus Christ, the Trinity, and the atoning death of Christ as God's sacrifice for sins. Evangelicals are serious about these matters and strive to integrate them into their church life and worship.

Beyond that, however, evangelical worship in America is a "blooming, buzzing confusion" (to use William James' vivid description of nature). Let's go on a brief survey of the diversity of evangelical worship styles. A major metropolitan area of around a million people will probably have hundreds of evangelical churches. Many of their ministers will belong to an area evangelical ministers' association. Either individually or through their denominations many will belong to the National Association of Evangelicals or one of its local affiliates. Most will gladly join in with a Billy Graham evangelistic crusade. For the most part, the pastors of these churches know which churches within a few miles radius of their own are also evangelical and they will network with other evangelical pastors.

Diversity in Evangelical Worship Style

Suppose, now, that someone moves to this metropolitan area and wants to settle into an evangelical church but isn't committed to a particular denomination or tradition. Many evangelicals do consider themselves evangelical first and Baptist or Methodist or Presbyterian second. A lot of these seekers will select a church based largely on its worship style. So what choices do they have among the evangelical churches in a fairly large city?

Perhaps a few evangelical churches will use a formal liturgy that revolves around the church calendar. These are usually Episcopalian, Presbyterian, or Lutheran. In their theology they tend to stand out from the other churches in these mainstream denominations, but their worship might not be very different from their more liberal sister churches. The minister probably wears a robe and the chancel ("platform" area) is divided (pulpit and lectern). The worship service is probably fairly formal and unemotional. Everything that is going to happen is printed in the worship folder or in a book of worship. The prayers are probably written and the sermon text selected from a lectionary (a published set of Scripture passages tied to the church calendar). Different colors will be displayed in the sanctuary depending on the season of the church year — Advent, Easter, Pentecost, and so on. Worshipers will stand and sit and perhaps kneel in their pews (on a padded kneeling railing that pulls down from the pew in front). There will be little or no spontaneity in the worship; everything is prescribed.

At the other end of the spectrum one will find evangelical churches that shun all vestiges of formal liturgy and revel in informality and spontaneity in worship. Such a church may have no written order of worship; the worship leader and/or pastor will set the pace and routine of worship "as the Spirit leads." Room will probably be left for congregants to participate with a testimony or prayer. Such evangelical worship usually includes lively singing of gospel songs and hymns; a "special musical number" sung by a soloist, duet, or trio; perhaps a choir selection (but not an anthem); and a sermon expounding the Scriptures and calling for people to accept Jesus Christ. Many such evangelical worship services end with an "altar call" or "invitation." People are invited to walk forward and pray with the pastor or with other church leaders (deacons or elders). Sometimes congregants are invited to kneel in their pews (not on a padded kneeling rail!) or at the "altar" (front of the sanctuary) to pray.

Between the extremely formal and liturgical and the revivalistic styles of worship lie many combinations and moderate styles. An entire spectrum of evangelical worship styles exists. An evangelical church may use what is called "blended worship," which incorporates elements of liturgy and contemporary "praise and worship" singing. Others will lock into just the contemporary style led by a loud band singing relatively recent contemporary Christian songs written by superstars of Christian recording. Still others will sing only hymns from a hymnal with organ accompaniment.

The variety and diversity of evangelical worship are immense; almost nothing beyond the five marks subtly blended in can be taken for granted. Is there a worship style that is incompatible with authentic evangelical faith? Not really. There may be elements of a church's worship that would make most evangelicals raise their eyebrows and wonder, but almost anything can be part of an evangelical worship service—dance, film, drama, Gregorian chant, saxophone, pipe organ, hellfire and brimstone preaching, lecture style sermon using PowerPoint, hand clapping to music, raising hands, contemplative prayer (using what is called *lectio divina*—spiritual reading of Scripture combined with meditation), banners, bare walls, shouting, or silence.

"Conservative Worship" Takes Different Appearances

So what is conservative evangelical worship and how is it possible to be authentically evangelical without being conservative in worship? Here, unlike in other chapters, we have to admit that there are no even relatively stable "conservative characteristics." A church may be conservative in its worship style by conserving traditional worship. But what that traditional worship looks like will differ from one denominational heritage to another. A Pentecostal church's worship may be conservative by shunning contemporary praise and worship chorus-singing to guitars and drums and using only piano and gospel songs from a book. An Episcopalian church's worship may be conservative by using an old version of the *Book of Common Prayer*, the unifying worship book of all Anglicans worldwide. Its worship may be polar opposite of the Pentecostal church's worship and yet both can be "conservative" in their own ways by being traditional and resistant to change. Thus, a conservative evangelical worship service may look, sound, and feel very different in one church than in another.

There's another element to throw into this already confusing mix. Many conservative evangelical churches are rushing into experimentation with worship styles to attract younger people and spiritual seekers who might be turned off by high church liturgy or hymn singing. One simply cannot judge how conservative a church is by its style of worship. That style may not look, sound, or feel conservative while the church may be using it precisely because it is a conservative evangelical church. Many of the praise and worship songs used in contemporary worship exalt Jesus, the cross, holy living, conservative values, witnessing to others about Jesus, and glorifying God above all else.

Some conservative evangelical churches believe that traditional worship styles suffocate spiritual fervor and drive a new generation away. Worship needs to be passionate and, yes, entertaining. A generation raised on MTV has a hard time sitting through a sedate service of worship with hymns and written prayers and a lengthy sermon expounding a passage of Scripture using insights from the Hebrew or Greek. Some conservative evangelical churches, then, embark on seemingly unfettered experimentation with worship styles precisely because they believe it is the best way to promote their traditional beliefs, practices, and experiences to a new generation.

One of the notable features of evangelical life in America is what is known as the "worship wars." What is called contemporary Christian worship began in the era of the Jesus Movement—the early 1970s. Jesus People sang choruses with guitar accompaniment. The choruses were often drawn from Scripture passages and rather than telling a story, expressing an aspiration, or urging a certain kind of living, they expressed praise to God for his wonderful grace and greatness. The Jesus People's influence on worship spread out from California (where the movement began at Calvary Chapel in Costa Mesa) across the country. By the late 1970s and early 1980s thousands of evangelical churches were laying down the hymnbooks and teaching their congregations praise and worship choruses written and recorded by Larry Norman or Keith Green. Then, later, came Chris Tomlin, Matt Redman, and others.

The choruses are usually displayed on a large screen or TV monitors at the front of the auditorium or sanctuary. They are sung with the help of a "praise team," often accompanied by a band with bass guitars, drums, and other musical instruments. In churches deeply influenced by this new wave of worship, choirs disappeared along with hymnbooks. Often the congregation stands and sings choruses repeatedly with outstretched or upheld arms and closed eyes. It can be very loud.

The reaction to this trend in evangelical worship has been dramatic and often divisive. Especially older evangelical worshipers will complain about the unfamiliar choruses and the lengthy sessions of standing while singing. They want to return to the hymns and gospel songs of their tradition. Evangelical churches have sometimes dealt with this division by having two or more worship services—one traditional (populated mostly by people fifty and older) and one contemporary (populated largely by young people). As a result, many evangelical churches are split into two congregations who rarely see each other. Others are critical of this approach to resolving the worship wars and yet do not want to settle into a stale traditionalism or launch into unfettered experimentation that trivializes worship by making it entertaining to the youth.

The question here, then, is how a person or a church can be authentically evangelical in worship without being conservative or trivializing worship. Some evangelical churches are conservative in worship by resisting innovation and warmly embracing tradition. There's nothing wrong with that. But other theologically conservative evangelical churches experiment with new styles of worship unfettered by any tradition or accountability. I have more of a problem with that, yet that's where many evangelical churches are going. Why do so many theologically conservative churches rush into experimental forms of worship when that seems like such a nonconservative thing to do? On the surface it doesn't seem consistent with being conservative.

My hunch is that many conservative churches risk trivializing worship because they are so passionate about reaching the younger generation with the gospel of Jesus Christ. Evangelism is important to them, and so is promoting their conservative values and lifestyles. They find the best way to attract young people who may never otherwise darken the door of a church is to cater to their tastes in music and make worship entertaining. But usually they haven't stopped to consider whether this is consistent with their conservative approach to doctrine and theology or whether it risks trivializing worship.

My overall thesis about worship is simply that there are no valid or invalid worship styles; a church can be authentically evangelical and worship in virtually any way as long as its worship is guided by the five hallmarks of evangelical faith. Worship style is a matter of personal taste and preference. The Bible does not prescribe any particular worship style.

The closest passage to such a prescription appears in 1 Corinthians 14:26: "When you come together, each one has a hymn, a lesson, a revelation, a tongue, or an interpretation. Let all things be done for edification." Pentecostals can take heart from this passage as it seems to endorse or at least recognize their preferred style of worship. Others argue that this was not meant to be a prescription for Christian worship forever but only a description of what believers were doing in the Corinthian church. The early second-century Christian writing known as *The Didache* describes and prescribes a more formal worship service, but even it is not highly liturgical and one wonders if it was meant for one group of Christians or all Christians everywhere. In any case, there is no single "biblical" form or style of worship.

Christians have worshiped in many different ways throughout the centuries. The Eastern Orthodox family of churches relies on a tradition of liturgical worship going back to the era of Roman Emperor Justinian and the development of worship in the Hagia Sophia cathedral in Constantinople (now Istanbul). Some describe it as "bells and smells" because it includes bell ringing and incense. Christians such as the Anabaptists during the Reformation worshiped informally with no liturgy. Evangelicals reflect that diversity. Theology cannot dictate how evangelicals ought to worship so long as their worship is truly evangelical — gospel-centered and influenced by *biblicism, conversionism, crucicentrism, activism,* and *respect for the Great Tradition of Christian doctrine.*

Anyone who claims that one particular style of worship is "best" had better be ready to explain what that means. "Best" by what standards? It's ironic that the worship wars among evangelicals have probably been the most divisive issue affecting them while the Bible is relatively silent about right worship (except that it edify everyone present), and diversity of worship has always existed at least since the Reformation.

One can be thoroughly and authentically evangelical and worship in virtually any way, using any style. So, there is no need to be conservative or "liberal" (experimental). While I am dismayed by the loss of the great hymns that used to serve as doctrinal training for young Christians, I do not think a hymnal is necessary for good worship. Even singing is not necessary although evangelicals have always loved to sing in worship. Too often older evangelicals have longed nostalgically for the "good old days" when worship was "better" because it was more staid and sedate and centered around traditional music and a topical sermon. To them (and I am sometimes one of them) I say, "Move over and make room for a younger generation to shape worship their way. Trust them, even as your elders trusted you to reshape worship."

When I was a kid, much evangelical worship was controversial because it was beginning to incorporate musical instruments other than piano and organ. One church banned saxophones from the sanctuary because of their association with jazz and nightclubs! But that didn't deter the younger people of the 1950s and 1960s who were intent on updating worship with new songs written by Ralph Carmichael and John Peterson. Older people of that generation often detested the new music and the introduction of jazzy instruments. When I was a teenager in the 1960s our Youth for Christ club sold contemporary Christian music vinyl albums door-to-door to raise money for YFC. The album jacket had so-called "psychedelic" lettering—reminiscent of the hippies and drug culture. So, people complained and YFC had to remove the album from circulation. The music was slow and sedate by today's standards, but it was upbeat and exciting to teenagers then.

My generation chafed at their elders repressing our tastes in music and worship. Now we are the "older generation" that tends to complain about the prevalence of the newer "praise and worship" choruses in church. What goes around comes around! Some evangelical churches are being conservative by enshrining a past form of worship as the only valid one for all times. A problem with that is that the past form of worship so dearly loved and clung to was new and controversial at one time. Isn't the older generation simply trying to impose their own taste on younger people? Probably so.

The one objective criterion for judging worship is the message. What words are being sung and why? What theology do they convey? What picture of God do they impress on the minds of worshipers? Are their messages biblical and God-honoring? These are more important questions than whether the songs are new or old, lively or sedate, choruses or hymns.

Much contemporary worship is simply trivial because it aims more at entertainment than real worship. Worship is ascribing worth to God; it revolves around the glory of God and his worthiness to be praised. Some contemporary worship does that, but much imitates the music of MTV or other secular music media or groups. Such churches need to examine their worship to decide if everything being done is for the glory of God and the edification of everyone or whether some of it is simply trendy and titillating.

I used to be a hymn singer only. Oh, choruses were fine for Sunday evening services, camps and retreats, but on Sunday morning the songs should be right out of the hymnal. I loved (and still love!) the hymns of Charles Wesley and the gospel songs of Charles Gabriel. For years I had my classes open sessions with prayer and a hymn that went along with the subject of study for the day or week. I saw it as my task to drag young people kicking and screaming (if necessary) back to the hymns of the church. I still think my motive had some validity; hymns pass the faith along from generation to generation in a way choruses don't.

Then, during a life crisis, I discovered the Southern gospel songs of my childhood and fell in love with the Gaither Homecoming tapes, CDs, videos, and DVDs. I have nearly all of them. For about ten years that was all I listened to, and I loved to sing along to the bouncy strains of "I'll Fly Away" or "I Woke Up This Morning Feelin' Fine." I even inflicted some of this on my students! Then I discovered contemporary Christian music. I had listened to what was then contemporary music in the 1960s and somewhat in the 1970s. In fact, I promoted one of the first Petra concerts back in the 1970s when that prototypical Christian rock band was new.

During the early years of the 2000s I returned to contemporary Christian music, but now it was today's CCM — Tree63 and Casting Crowns! Fantastic stuff. But I recognize validity in every stage of my peripatetic musical wanderings. It's all a matter of taste and what God can use to inspire. Of course, through it all I paid close attention to messages and discerned the difference between "good" and "bad" Christian music by the gospel and the glory of God. I've decided what I long knew was right — Christian music is largely a matter of taste. As long as the words bring glory to God and promote the gospel of Jesus Christ, all is well. I now look back and recognize all the stages of my journey with Christian music as valid. No genre is better or worse than another. I can even appreciate Christian rap!

How to be evangelical without being conservative in worship? Two prescriptions come to mind. First, prepare to change worship styles and allow God to speak through unfamiliar forms and music. Don't baptize any style of worship or musical genre as the one and only for all times and places. Resist the hardening of the categories that tends to set in with age; bring youthful music and worship into the churches without letting down all standards of discernment. Discern the difference between "good" and "bad" worship and music by the criteria of the glory of God and the gospel.

Second, value tradition in worship. Strictly avoid trendiness and entertainment. Don't throw the baby out with the bathwater when updating worship; hold on to what is good and right from the past and give it new clothes. A model of this is Christian musician Fernando Ortega, who takes old hymns and gospel songs and refurbishes them for a younger generation.

Objective Criteria for Evangelical Worship

So what objective criteria can help evangelicals determine what is good worship? Any style or approach to worship is valid so long as it glorifies God and helps us enjoy him. The first question and answer of the Westminster Shorter Catechism is, "What is the chief end of man? The chief end of man is to glorify God and enjoy him forever." That should be the chief end of worship as well. It doesn't matter whether it is fast or slow, loud or quiet, old or new, liturgical or informal—as long as it focuses on God and his glory and helps us revel in his greatness and goodness.

Thoughtless worship that either adheres to tradition or rushes into experimentation and entertainment trivializes worship. But one cannot attribute worth to God in a trivial manner, so "trivialized worship" is an oxymoron. And yet much evangelical worship is trivialized because it is not intentionally focused on God's glory and the worshiping community's enjoyment of God. It isn't form that trivializes worship but routine. And it isn't contemporaneity that trivializes worship but unfettered experimentation and entertainment. Neither being conservative by uncritically holding onto traditional forms of worship or uncritically experimenting with "contemporary worship" out of desire to attract young people is consistent with an authentically evangelical worship experience. What is necessary is careful thought and reflection on how all the elements of worship come together to magnify and glorify God and lift up the worshiping community into his presence.

169

::CHAPTER 11

ACCEPTING WITHOUT AFFIRMING
FLAWED PEOPLE

Some years ago the book *I'm Okay, You're Okay* (HarperPaper-backs, 2004) caused quite a stir in conservative evangelical circles. Well, perhaps it wasn't the book itself so much as the title that caused the controversy. And maybe it wasn't so much a controversy as a feast of making fun of the title. Some wag invented a bumper sticker that said, "I'm Okay, But I Don't Know About You." That was inevitable.

Many conservative evangelical preachers and evangelists heaped scorn on the book's title as a motto for the self-esteem movement stemming mainly from California and sweeping the nation. They saw the book as a symbol of the "relational revolution" that emphasized self-acceptance as the path toward accepting other people. The relational revolution, which included a number of Christian authors and speakers, sought to go beyond self-forgiveness and tolerance of others to a deeper level of true acceptance without the perfectionist impulse to try to change everyone — including oneself. The goal was true community, but many conservative evangelicals saw the movement as humanistic and a secular search for salvation. Especially those outside evangelical churches were considered anything but "okay."

Flawed People Everywhere —
Even in Every Church

Of course, as with every chapter in this book, it's important to say that not every evangelical who considers himself or herself conservative is guilty of trashing the relational revolution, *I'm Okay, You're Okay*, or self-esteem therapy. They are certainly not opposed to true community. But in the popular mind, conservative evangelicals as a group are regarded as exclusive and intolerant because of their drawing of boundaries around themselves to keep out the flagrant sinners of secular society around them.

To what extent that's a stereotype is hard to say. Growing up in conservative evangelicalism I have to confess that I picked up the attitude that there's something risky if not unchristian about having non-Christian friends. And as for homosexuals and other people living blatantly sinful lifestyles, well, we knew to shun them unless and until they changed. Moreover, some of my conservative evangelical acquaintances expressed belief that homosexuals could not change and should be kept away from churches and especially young people.

Conservative evangelicals have not come very far in tolerating sinners since I was a young person growing up in an evangelical church. Back then, we gladly welcomed sinners into our midst to win them to Christ, but we didn't welcome them into our fellowship. We knew something we tried hard not to let them know. They could be among us and receive our prayers and spiritual counseling for a long time without changing, but unless they gave up sinning they would never really be one of us. They would never enter into our circle of brothers and sisters in Christ. But later I came to wonder what we meant by their giving up sinning. Was it just that we knew about their sins? Did we expect them to give up their known sinful habits while we could keep our secret ones?

You see, the problem was, as a pastor's kid I knew — because I snuck around and listened carefully to my parents' private conversations — that many of the pillars of our church and denomination were secretly living sinful lifestyles. Occasionally they would be disciplined by someone higher up, but often their secret sins were simply accepted as part of their struggle to live for God. It seemed to me a double standard was in operation. A minister who was caught in adultery was thrown out of the denomination while a minister who wasn't caught but many suspected that he was living a secret, sinful life was allowed to stay in the fellowship. And church members who confessed their secret sinful habits to the pastor or an elder were often counseled and given a great deal of freedom to keep functioning within the body of Christ even as visitors (to say nothing of neighbors who didn't visit!) were treated as pariahs behind their backs until they gave up smoking, drinking, dancing, cursing, extramarital sex, or gambling.

Let me give an example. Our assistant pastor's wife became involved in an extramarital affair. I knew it because I heard my parents talking about it at home. But nothing happened to her except that my mother went to her home to pray with her frequently. She attended church through it all as if nothing was wrong. She taught Sunday school and participated in every church activity even though many people knew she was cheating on her husband. She and her husband and their family were solidly plugged into the church and casting her out would have been a terrible scandal and probably would have caused some division in the congregation. Eventually she did stop the affair, so far as I recall, but I'm not sure anything would have happened if she hadn't.

Another woman visited the church many times and was known to virtually everyone in the congregation as practically a prostitute. She wasn't married, but slept with various men. (Again, I knew this because my parents talked about such things carelessly thinking I wasn't paying any attention.) She was allowed to visit, but not really participate even though she clearly wanted to change and needed the church's help to change. Even as a twelve-year-old child I wondered whether she could change as long as she was kept out of the center of the church's fellowship and treated as a vile person.

Over the years I've noticed this apparent double standard in conservative evangelical churches; in the name of "holiness" they tend to hold at arm's length people who admit their sins and seek help until they are "delivered" (as Pentecostals say) or "give up their sin" (as Baptists say). They aren't invited into the inner circle of true believers until their "besetting sin" is either compartmentalized and kept secret or they really do stop whatever it is. (I suspect in many cases it is the former!) All the while, other people already in the full fellowship of true believers are allowed to live scandalous lives. The line is often drawn with sexual sins. A pillar of the church might be disciplined in some way for flagrant or discovered sexual sin, but is allowed to practice gluttony, spousal abuse, shady financial dealing, conspicuous consumption, or lying about others within the church. Sometimes even sexual sin is swept under the rug.

I don't want to give the wrong impression here. I'm not accusing conservative evangelicals of conscious, willful hypocrisy. That's usually not the case. But with good intentions many of them practice a double standard for those already within the fellowship of true believers who are all sinners and those outside the fellowship looking in. Many conservative evangelicals say that we are all flawed people, including the "best Christians" — but some are apparently more flawed than others. Outsiders' flaws are worse than insiders' flaws. No doubt that's one reason it's difficult to break into the fellowship of many conservative evangelical churches; newcomers are expected to change while longtime attenders and members are given greater latitude to remain flawed.

A Dilemma and Wrong Solutions

So where am I going with this? If my admittedly dismal portrait of too many conservative evangelical communities bears some resemblance to reality, which I think is the case, what should be done about it? How can evangelicals become more honest, open, and real about sinful people inside, outside, and on the margins of their churches? I suspect that the problem I'm pointing out is one many conservative evangelicals have simply come to accept for lack of a solution. They can't let down their standards of holy conduct, but neither can they expel everyone in the church who is sinning on a regular basis and not really overcoming their besetting sins.

Two wrong solutions have been tried. Some evangelical churches have simply given up on holiness and church discipline and decided to "leave it to the Lord" to judge people's lives. These churches have found a solution by abolishing boundaries; people aren't even asked about their lifestyles when they come to join or hold leadership positions. The church turns a blind eye to even open, unrepentant sinning by inquirers and longtime members. It's between them and God. The only question is whether they want to go on a faith journey with this community of flawed but forgiven people. I wonder if such churches are really conservative or even evangelical. They certainly no longer fit any popular image of conservative evangelical.

The second wrong approach to the problem is to shore up the boundaries and denounce the flagrant sinners outside the church, on its margins, and inside the fellowship. My wife and I recently visited a conservative evangelical church where the pastor spent ten minutes at the end of his Sunday sermon on sin naming a relatively minor staff member who was caught viewing pornography and explaining that he was fired. I looked around the congregation and thought about the statistics claiming that almost half of all evangelical men — including ministers and church professionals — view Internet pornography. Was this staff member being disciplined and excluded only because he was caught? What would happen if everyone in the church who viewed pornography or allowed lustful thoughts and images to linger in his or her mind stood up and admitted it? I suspect that would include half or more of every church. What would be left if they were all excluded? Mostly elderly women?

It's easy to identify a problem, but it is much more difficult to come up with a solution. If these two solutions aren't good, what is a good solution? How should evangelical churches deal with flawed people? How can we uphold biblical standards of holiness without pretending that anyone is without sin? Put differently, how can we admit that we are all deeply flawed and sinful, and that most of us even have besetting sins with which we have pretty much come to terms, without erasing the boundaries between the church and the world?

A Suggestion for Resolving the Dilemma

I think one step toward solving that problem is for evangelicals to stop considering themselves "conservative." The label has such a serious and dour ring to it. It automatically suggests Puritanism especially within a religious context. Being conservative signals a desire and intention of somehow or other enforcing traditional standards of moral and ethical conduct. Often those standards are drawn from a different era.

Conservative evangelicals are notorious for lapsing a couple decades or more behind everyone else when it comes to accepting behaviors as normal. Many evangelicals were pacifists until World War II or the Korean War. Many used to shun television and movies. Most used to avoid dancing, to say nothing of drinking alcohol even in the form of a glass of wine with a meal! Today many even conservative evangelicals think nothing of those behaviors, but they are still harshly judgmental about sexual sins and paradoxically lenient about gluttony and shady business practices. Yet conservative evangelicals still tend to exclude people who don't fit a certain mold of holiness. There are inevitable boundary markers of conduct that keep people out of the center of the fellowship unless and until they change.

So what direction should evangelical churches take in this regard? How should we treat flawed people, both those among us and those who seek to join us who struggle with sin? I'm not asking about the inevitable little old man or lady in the church who admits to having a "problem" with gossip. I'm asking about the person who struggles with homosexuality or serial adultery or gluttony or alcoholism or lying. Such people are already in the churches — among us. That's what evangelicals need to wake up to and admit openly to themselves. We are a group of people little different in our lifestyles from the world around us. We're just much better at hiding our flaws—especially if they are the ones our churches condemn as especially heinous.

Thus, my second prescription for being evangelical but not conservative with regard to flawed people is to admit that nobody is free from some besetting sin in the form of a bad habit—whether a pattern of lying or viewing pornography or stealing from an employer or cheating employees out of a fair wage or verbally abusing the spouse and children or severe temper flareups or compulsive gambling or eating or drinking to excess. As evangelicals we do believe that God can change people, but most of us don't believe that anyone can become perfectly free from every sinful habit or pattern of life. Nor must we expect seekers to behave as we claim to, but often don't, in order to be among us. Instead of "I'm okay; you're okay," or "I'm okay, but I don't know about you," evangelicals should embrace as our motto: "You're not okay, but neither are we."

In other words, we need to become real about people and sin. We need to stop expecting holiness of life while keeping it as an impossible ideal we all should strive for. Only God is holy; our holiness comes from Jesus Christ, whose righteousness is given to us as a gift by God when we repent and trust in him by clinging to his cross as our only hope for salvation. I don't think we can claim to "have" holiness or even "be holy." But we can participate in God's holiness by virtue of the indwelling of the Holy Spirit that brings union with Christ. How? By radical faith in Jesus Christ.

Evangelicals know all this; it's common talk among us. But some seem to forget that our only righteousness is God's and we can only receive it by faith in Jesus Christ; we have no righteousness of our own. Our only merit before God is his, through the cross. We expect people to be saved by faith alone but then overcome sin by hard effort. That effort might be disciplining the will (Baptist version) or tarrying to receive the infilling of the Holy Spirit (Pentecostal). Whatever it may be, however, it is work, and we expect seekers who want to join our fellowship to do it and become morally upright in appearance if not in reality.

Becoming real about people and sin means admitting to ourselves and everyone that we are all sinners. Oh, we evangelicals do that. But do we really mean it? Too often not, I fear. When we say "we are all sinners," do we really mean that every one of us has some besetting sin not yet overcome in our life? If we really mean that, which is doubtful, then we should act as if that were the case. That means blurring the boundaries between the sinners in the church and the sinners outside the church and being more welcoming of the flawed people who come to our church doors because they are really not that much different from us. We evangelicals say that we hate sin but love the sinner. But is that a glib cliché? Do we want to be around sinners? Do we feel at home with them? Do we want them among us? Probably not. Too often we are a holy club rather than a hospital for the sinful.

Perhaps it's time to go beyond "love the sinner but hate the sin" and simply become accepting of sinners — as Jesus was. That's not the same as affirming the sin. Jesus never did that, nor should we. We can't do that and remain evangelicals. But we can be authentically evangelical and move beyond the conservative attitude that our job is to uphold traditional morality by excluding people who have sin in their lives. And perhaps we should reexamine the Bible to see whether some of the things we have taught as sin really are sins or whether they are our boundary markers to distinguish ourselves from the world. And perhaps we should reexamine the Bible to see whether some of the things we have not called sin really are sins. If we do that, we will definitely find out that most of us within evangelical churches still have sin in our lives.

Jesus located sin in the heart; attitudes and dispositions are the primary sins. Money is not the root of all sin but love of money is. Sex is not sinful, but craving sex with anyone other than one's spouse is sinful. But who, then, is without sin? Ah, nobody. Wasn't that Jesus' point? But we evangelicals have often fallen into the trap of pretending that people can and do rise above all besetting sins by identifying sin only with certain practices we either can hide well or are not particularly drawn to.

In other words, the second prescription for evangelicals is to get real about people and sin by acknowledging the universality of sin and dropping the pretense that some of us are without any really bad sins in our lives. There is no line between "them" and "us" when it comes to being sinners. There is a line, but it doesn't lie between sin and no sin; it lies between attitudes toward sin.

My third prescription for evangelicals is to focus less on people's behavior and more on their attitudes toward sin. In other words, does a person who is sinning (which is everyone) acknowledge sin in his or her life? Does the person name sinful behavior as sin or does the person try to hide it or rationalize it as not really sinful? Does the person want to be delivered from it even if he or she is not yet being delivered from it?

Let's take alcoholism as an example. Why can't we evangelicals simply acknowledge that there are alcoholics among us? I personally know of some well-known evangelicals who have struggled with that demon in their lives. But they struggled with it alone and secretly, or they have left their evangelical churches and either dropped church altogether or drifted off into some liberal, "inclusive" church that doesn't care about such sins. Wouldn't it be so much better if an alcoholic evangelical could publicly acknowledge that "this is my demon with which I struggle; please help me"? Yet that will only work if everyone does it. If statistics hold true, evangelicals are just as likely to be alcoholics as people in the nonevangelical population. The same could be said of marital struggles, divorces, homosexuality, adultery, lying, and gluttony.

Examples of the New Approach

Let me offer a model of how this might work. I know a fine evangelical person who has been a church professional for many years. She has served on pastoral staffs of churches, taught in evangelical colleges and universities, and is to many people a stellar example of an "on fire for God" evangelical leader. She spends most of her free time helping the poor and especially poor children. She chooses intentionally to live among the poor when her salary would easily allow her to live comfortably in the suburbs. She and I agree on this matter of becoming real about sin.

One Sunday morning it was her turn to give the testimony of the week. She revealed a sinful habit from which God had freed her. But then she told of her current struggle with binge eating to relieve anxiety. To her, that is a sin and God hasn't yet delivered her from it. To her way of thinking everyone sitting in that evangelical congregation struggles with some sin. After all, we are all, as she likes to say, "pond scum." (Like all good evangelicals she believes in original sin and total depravity.) But we are God-loved pond scum. Christ died for us pond scum. She asked the congregation to pray for her to be freed from her use of food as a crutch to handle anxiety and depression.

What she did took courage, but I dare say most people sitting there listening to her were little shocked. After all, as affluent Americans we're accustomed to gluttony; we don't really consider it a sin. We know it is, but we have become comfortable with it. Except her. I'm willing to bet that most people sitting in the pews hearing her were thinking, "Oh, if people here only knew what *my* struggle with sin is like! It's much worse than that!" Someone over there near that stained glass window secretly drinks too much and occasionally becomes drunk but has learned to cover it up so that nobody but his spouse knows. Another person back by the doors slinks into church every Sunday regretting that he viewed Internet pornography again yesterday. Yet another person is thinking about her life long struggle with anger that occasionally explodes into fits of rage where she curses her children and beats them.

What if everyone felt safe, if not comfortable, to get up and reveal his or her besetting sin and ask the congregation to pray for God's deliverance? What if we all took off our masks and let others see our flaws? What if confession of sin to one another became the norm so that people who did *not* confess their sins were considered a problem for the church? What if evangelical churches dropped the pretense that anyone has fully recovered from addiction to any and every sin? What if our churches really became hospitals for sinners rather than clubs for saints? People with family problems wouldn't have to stay away from church for fear of being judged. People with sinful habits could come to church to get help and hopefully healing. We could all stop pretending and be real about our true conditions. We would be stronger communities because we would all be in the struggle against sin together.

I know a pastor who stood in the pulpit with his wife on a Sunday morning and revealed that they were having marital problems and were in weekly marital counseling. He didn't sugarcoat it but told the congregation it was bad and without intervention they would probably get a divorce. That week many couples in that congregation sought professional help to save their marriages. That church turned a corner and began to be known as a place where sinners could attend and participate as long as they didn't cover up or deny their sinfulness.

What I'm proposing isn't a totally new idea. During the height of the Jesus People Movement in the early 1970s I worked in a Christian coffeehouse ministry. There we talked a lot about "transparency" and created an atmosphere where people could hang out among Christians even as they struggled with drug and sex addictions. Nobody was judged unfit to participate as long as they didn't claim to be holy. That was not unique; many Jesus People ministries were like that.

I recall one evening when the pastor of the church that operated the coffeehouse and his wife were there. They were sitting sipping coffee with a newly saved young couple who looked like hippies. They weren't married yet, but were living together. The long-haired young man asked the pastor and his wife, "Were you virgins when you got married?" I overheard the question and leaned in closely to hear the answer. It was noncommittal and I was disappointed. That wasn't the atmosphere we nurtured in the coffeehouse. It wasn't transparency.

Many conservative evangelicals would say, "That was an inappropriate question." In most evangelical settings it would be.

But that's the problem. Probably half of all evangelical married couples weren't both virgins when they got married. So what? I'm certainly not advocating condoning sex before marriage, but I am proposing we drop the pretense that good evangelicals don't do such things. They do. Pretending that they don't do such things fosters an atmosphere that is closed to sinners. It promotes self-righteousness and denial.

Leaving Denial Behind

So, am I recommending that evangelicals lower their moral and ethical standards in order to become more inclusive? No. I'm recommending that we raise our moral and ethical standards and encourage everyone to admit their struggles with sin so that both the church and the world know what ideals they strive for but also that they do not claim to have arrived. Raising moral and ethical standards means including among the list of sins those with which evangelicals have become comfortable: gluttony, gossip, greed, racism, sexism, uncontrolled anger, and bitterness. Encouraging everyone to admit their struggles with these and other sins means insisting that people name their sins as sins and not claim to have arrived at a spiritual plane higher and better than others who struggle with different sins. Being inclusive means accepting flawed people who are willing to admit they are flawed and sinful as long as they are willing to call their sins sins and not excuse or deny them.

Let's consider a difficult example. What about homosexuality? For some reason conservative evangelicals have latched on to this issue as a kind of Caesar's Rubicon across which they will not go. In other words, they will not accept homosexual behavior as normal or "okay" as many in the world around them insist they do. As a result of their loud condemnations of homosexual behavior, homosexuals have felt excluded unless they keep their inclinations and actions secret. Some leave the evangelical church because they are made to feel their besetting sin (e.g., of fantasizing about having sex with someone of the same gender if not actually doing it) is especially heinous. Others keep it secret for the same reason.

Few evangelical churches have managed to handle this problem well. All well-read evangelical leaders know that many ministers and laypeople in their churches are homosexuals and at least occasionally act out those impulses. As long as they keep it secret, they're okay. But people who eat to excess so that they ruin their health feel no such criticism; they can be quite open about their "problem" without fear of being named a sinner and excluded.

I suggest that evangelicals accept homosexuals just as they accept gluttons. Usually the latter are included as long as they don't defend their behaviors as okay. In other words, as long as they don't trumpet their "lifestyle" as normal and declare they have no intention to change, they are usually given a place in the fellowship. It is possible to accept flawed and sinful people who admit their sins and seek God's help to overcome them without affirming their sins. In fact, that is where we must go — in the direction of being completely open and honest about every sin that exists and accepting sinners into fellowship without affirming their/our sinfulness as okay.

In other words, the reason a practicing homosexual (or an alcoholic) should not be included fully in the fellowship of evangelical Christians is that they deny their behavior is sinful or that they are flawed people in that area of life. If they do, however, admit it, name their sin as sin, and seek help to overcome it, they should be accepted like any other member of the fellowship — all of whom struggle with sin. The problem is not being a sinner, which we all are; the problem is calling evil good. But, don't we accept that also? How many times have conservative evangelicals celebrated war as if it were not a necessary evil but something good — as long as our side wins?

Belong, Believe, Then Behave

What I am suggesting is that evangelicals adopt a different habit regarding membership in the body of Christ. In the past and present most conservative evangelicals require that people believe, behave, and then belong or behave, believe, and then belong. Instead, I'm suggesting that we allow people who really do want to join the fellowship to belong, then believe and behave. Of course, nobody believes perfectly or behaves perfectly. If we require perfect belief and behavior, who could join?

But should we lower all expectations so that anyone can belong without restrictions? No. Perhaps everyone who wishes to belong should be required to confess that he or she is a sinner forgiven by God's grace and accepted by his mercy and wants to be changed by God's power. They should also confess, "Lord, I believe; help thou my unbelief." Then they should promise to embark on an accountable journey of faith and discipleship toward holiness together with all the other sinners.

Am I advocating a complete abdication of the church's responsibility to be a holy people separated to God? No. What separates people from God more than anything else is self-righteousness and having to practice sin in secrecy. I'm advocating becoming real about sin and trusting God to empower people to rise above sin. And I'm arguing that the church should continue to name sin as sin—including every sin and not just the ones we evangelicals tend to single out as especially heinous.

What should be done, then, about the person who belongs to the evangelical fellowship but continues in sin without apparent remorse or progress toward amendment of life? The same policy and practice should be adopted as in the Alcoholics Anonymous organization. People should be allowed to attend and struggle with help from a mentor-discipler and the entire body of Christ so long as they really want that help and are willing to admit they need it. But a deceiver who wants to belong for ulterior motives should be asked to reconsider his or her status as a member and ultimately be expelled without any evidence of desire to change. Church discipline is important, but it should be done with mercy and the goal of restoration.

::CHAPTER 12

PRACTICING EQUALITY WITHOUT SACRIFICING DIFFERENCE

Our family needed to find a new church to attend, so we visited one of our denomination in a nearby city. We went knowing the pastor was a woman and wondering what that would be like. Both my wife and I were a bit wary, but we were open to having a female pastor because we couldn't think of any biblical reason against it. Still, we weren't sure if we would like it. During the morning worship service God clearly spoke to both of us, telling us this was the church for us. The fact that the pastor was a woman made no difference to how the service went; if anything the sermon had a special feeling of grace. On the way home for Sunday lunch we were both silent. After eating we opened up to teach other about what we were hearing from God. The message was the same: God wanted us to move to this church even though it was not in our own city.

After a few weeks attending our new church we began to see why we were led there. Our middle school daughter had trouble fitting in with the youth group at our previous church; the youth group there was filled with problems. We watched as our daughter began to fit in with her new youth group and grow spiritually. We were joyful when she chose to be baptized by the youth pastor.

Some evangelicals would deny that God wanted us to go to that church—merely because the pastor was a woman. Yet we experienced God there in a very special way. It wasn't just a subjective "feeling." Both my wife and I knew God was speaking to us to go there—perhaps for our daughter's sake. All of us experienced spiritual refreshing there and the woman pastor was a key part of that.

When the denomination published its annual book of churches and pastors, it listed our pastor's husband as the church's pastor. We never knew why, but we suspected it was in deference to those in the denomination who opposed women in ministry.

The contemporary evangelical community has unfortunately divided into two competing camps over the issue of gender roles and equality between men and women. One camp has called its view "complementarianism." In other words, the two genders complement one another even though their roles are different. To others this seems like a semantic subterfuge because the leading complementarian evangelicals argue that women should be subordinate to men in families, churches, and society. The other camp also believes in the complementarity of the sexes, but they argue that men and women are absolutely equal in every respect, especially with regard to authority in home, church, and society. They call their view "egalitarianism" or "biblical equality."

Of course, the conservative evangelicals who belong to or sympathize with the Biblical Council on Manhood and Womanhood (the main complementarian organization) also claim they believe in equality of men and women, but they hold that men's roles include authority over women and women's roles include subordination to men's authority. To egalitarians this hardly sounds like equality because true equality requires equal rights and at least a balance of power.

Beyond Equality to Interdependence

Often when two groups face off over an issue of power and rights, each side loses sight of something important. The tendency to throw the baby out with the bathwater is almost irresistible. Complementarians tend to throw the baby of women's equal rights out with what they see as the bathwater of modern, feminist dissolution of gender differences. Egalitarians tend to throw the baby of gender distinctions out with the bathwater of patriarchalism. Of course, egalitarians acknowledge certain basic differences between men and women; it is impossible to ignore or deny the biological or physiological differences. But at least some egalitarians want to downplay or minimize gender role distinctions. To many egalitarians males and females differ only with regard to biology (which is not destiny) and socially constructed roles. The whole idea of ontological gender distinctions that transcend anatomy is anathema because it raises the specter of inequality between males and females.

I propose that evangelicals learn to move beyond the debate over issues of equality, authority, and roles and focus more on the interdependence between men and women in every area of life. Acknowledgment of gender interdependence will lead to equality if it has not already been recognized and is not yet being practiced. Underlying human equality is human interdependence. People who truly need each other find it difficult to oppress each other. Men who realize their dependence on women will respect their dignity and honor their equal rights. Women who realize their dependence on men will likewise respect them and honor their rights.

Movements to assert equality, like movements to affirm hierarchy (viz., men over women), often lead to spiritual if not physical separation. Mainstream feminist theologians have founded the Women Church Movement with congregations in almost every major city in North America. An entire book of liturgies for Women Churches has been written by feminist theologian Rosemary Radford Ruether (*Women-Church: Theology and Practice of Feminist Liturgical Communities* [Harper & Row, 1986]). Some Women Churches welcome men to attend, but for the most part they are not allowed to hold leadership positions. This is an understandable overreaction to centuries of exclusion and oppression of women by men in church life.

More recently some churches have been founded for men only. Such churches target men who are disengaged with churches because they are too feminine. Even churches with male leaders can cater to women. Men's churches cater to men by keeping services to no more than one hour and by omitting congregational singing (which men allegedly dislike).

The Enlightenment-inspired rage for personal rights and equal authority in every area of life has clearly invaded Christian churches. That is not to say anything against equal rights and equal authority, but hopefully these can be established, achieved, and practiced on the basis of biblical revelation and sound theological reasoning. And hopefully they can be achieved without separating the sexes into competing and sometimes even warring gender-specific religious movements.

Male/Female Complementarity

A place to begin is with the biblical theme of male/female complementarity. According to the Genesis stories of creation (Genesis 1 and 2) God pronounced everything he created good. But man (Adam) was not good alone; he needed woman (Eve). The New Testament emphasizes mutual submission between husbands and wives and speaks of the fact that in Christ there is "neither male nor female." Also, according to the New Testament, men and women, husbands and wives, are made for each other and should seek each other's good (see 1 Corinthians 7:3–4, 11:11–12; Ephesians 5:21; Galatians 3:28).

Genesis 1:27 makes clear that both men and women are created equally in God's image. In fact, the verse may reasonably be read to mean that neither one is fully in the image of God without the other. Christian theologians such as Karl Barth have argued that the image of God lies precisely in male/female complementarity and that the marriage relationship between two persons of different genders especially displays the image of God in humanity. That is not to say, of course, that unmarried persons are not fully in the image of God but only that their being in God's image requires that they relate to the opposite sex in mutual interdependence.

Egalitarian evangelicals have done all evangelicals (and others) a great service by highlighting the Bible's historically overlooked theme of equality between males and females and by demonstrating the reasonableness of interpreting the hierarchical passages as culturally conditioned. Evangelical theologians Stanley J. Grenz and Denise Muir Kjesbo did both in their excellent book *Women in the Church: A Biblical Theology of Women in Ministry* (Inter-Varsity Press, 1995). Complementarian evangelicals have done all Christians a service by underscoring the unassailable ontological distinctions between the genders that transcend mere physiology.

However, complementarians, most of who are conservative evangelicals, have failed to make a convincing case that women must submit to men's authority especially when men are wrong. And they have failed to convince many of us that only men should lead in families, churches, and society. Their argument overlooks the simple fact that truth, not office or role, is authoritative. If a woman has the truth, men should submit to that. Moreover, modern sociology has conclusively demonstrated that women tend to have ways of knowing truth that complement male ways of knowing truth. When it comes to knowing the truth, men and women depend on each other.

Egalitarian evangelicals have taken us a step beyond the entrenched conservatism that defends hierarchical patterns of relationships in marriage, church, and society. They have based their arguments not only on the Bible but also on history, which shows that during the nineteenth century evangelicals were in the forefront of American movements for equal rights for women. Donald Dayton's excellent book *Rediscovering an Evangelical Heritage* (Harper & Row, 1976) conclusively demonstrates this little-known chapter of evangelical history. Dayton's own Free Methodist Church was the first Christian denomination to ordain women, and it has always been solidly evangelical in terms of the four (or five) hallmarks of authentic evangelicalism spelled out in this book's introduction and in previous chapters.

Just as evangelicals were in the forefront of the movement to abolish slavery in Great Britain and America but tended to lag behind in civil rights for African Americans, so evangelicals were in the forefront of the movement to give women the vote and right to own property while lagging behind the rest of society in recognizing full equality of women with men in every area of society, including church life. The organization Christians for Biblical Equality has attempted to redress this neglect among contemporary evangelicals and promotes full equality between men and women without adopting the radical perspective of gender feminism that regards women as superior to men.

The Trouble with Complementarianism

Many evangelicals are simply impatient with the entrenched conservatism among many churches when it comes to practicing equality between different kinds of persons. Many of us find it simply silly when fellow evangelicals speak of an equality between men and women that is compatible with men having all the power and authority and women submitting "graciously" to men in every circumstance. Would even the most conservative evangelical complementarians give credence to such compatibility in the case of race relations? What if someone argued (as they have in the past) that whites and blacks are equal but whites should monopolize power and authority and blacks should "graciously" submit to white leadership? I believe evangelical complementarians would scoff at such "equality." Yet they dare to argue that their own hierarchical vision of male/female relationships is compatible with true equality.

Genuine justice, of which equality is a necessary ingredient, requires a balance of power. This insight was one of the greatest contributions of American theologian Reinhold Niebuhr and was taken up by Christian civil rights activists in the 1960s. Monopolies of power always corrupt and undermine justice by destroying real equality among persons. Even the best-intentioned husband will never treat his wife as equal with him in dignity as long as she is subject to him and he is not subject to her as well. Mutuality in submission is necessary to real equality. Equality requires power to challenge authority when it is wrong. Equality does not exist where power is held in the hands of one person in a relationship or in the hands of one group in a society.

As an evangelical who has belonged for ten years to two churches in a row pastored by women and as the father of two very independent-minded daughters who are on their own paths to success in life, I have grown impatient with continuing arguments over gender roles among evangelicals. I have experienced the divine calling and gifting of women in ministry. Both my birth mother and stepmother were licensed if not ordained ministers. The evangelical denomination in which I was raised ordained women and women ministered alongside men as pastors and evangelists. My female pastors have been two of the most spiritually gifted Christian leaders I have ever known and they have ministered to me and to my family with great ability and success.

I have occasionally been asked by conservative evangelicals when I became liberal and accepted the feminist viewpoint concerning women in ministry. I proudly reply that I have never held any other viewpoint although I have never considered it "feminist" or "liberal." To me, feminism is more than simply belief in and practice of equality of women with men; it is a belief system that tends to elevate typically female traits above male ones. It suggests that masculinity is corrupting and calls men and women to achieve a "feminized consciousness" that recognizes traditional women's ways of being in the world as better than men's. Some people call that "gender feminism," but it is so pervasive among feminist scholars that I now simply call it feminism.

I am not a feminist in that sense. And since that is the word's prevailing sense in the academic community at least, I cannot call myself a feminist at all. But I do believe in the full equality of women and men because I believe both are created equally in God's image and likeness and that Christ came equally for both. I also experience the reality that every healthy individual has both a female side or aspect and a male one. The two do not need to be in competition with each other; the two ways of living in the world complement each other. I experience the reality that as a man I am dependent on women and women are dependent on me and other men. We are mutually interdependent. Apart we are only partially human; together we are more fully human.

Does that make me liberal? I don't think so. But in terms of today's evangelicalism it makes me *not conservative*. Conservative evangelicals generally (with a few exceptions) oppose egalitarianism and interdependence between the genders. Their opposition to the former is explicit; their opposition to the latter is more implicit. The fact that only men can hold leadership roles in families and churches demonstrates the lack of interdependence in their view of gender relationships, whatever they may say with their lips or pens.

Of course, a person might argue that leaders are dependent on followers. True enough. But that's a different kind of dependence than real, biblical interdependence. Genuine interdependence requires mutual leadership of each other. It requires mutual submission. Parents may be dependent on their children emotionally, but they are rarely if ever said to be "dependent on their children." That's an abnormal way of speaking. Slave owners in the antebellum South may have been economically dependent on their slaves, but who would speak of their "slave dependence"? "Interdependence" of slave owners and slaves would be an odd expression.

True interdependence requires equality while transcending it. Whites and blacks can be equal without being interdependent. But the goal of healthy race relations in America is interdependence beyond equality. So between men and women interdependence transcends equality, and healthy male/female relations require interdependence.

An Example of Needing Balance

Let me illustrate by using one of the two female-pastored churches to which my wife and I have belonged. It is one of the finest churches we have ever known; its woman pastor has been the finest pastor of the many who have ministered to us in our almost thirty-five years of married life. This church is thoroughly evangelical in the sense of embodying the four or five hallmarks of authentic evangelicalism mentioned in the introduction: *biblicism, conversionism, crucicentrism, activism,* and *respect for the Great Tradition of Christian doctrine.*

Nevertheless, it cannot be called conservative because of the predominance of women on its pastoral staff and its proportion of female congregational leaders. It is more theologically conservative (in other respects) than many mainline Protestant churches in its vicinity. Unlike them, this congregation adheres to the authority of the Bible. The Bible stands at the center of all the church's teaching and decision-making. Membership in the church depends on genuine conversion to Christ by repentance and faith and testimony of the same. The cross of Jesus Christ is affirmed as the only way of salvation and the church is active in evangelism, missions, and social transformation. It adheres to the great doctrines of the Bible classically affirmed and confessed by Protestants since the Reformation.

However, this church's pastoral staff of seven includes four women. And women are the majority on both the governing board of the church and among the deacons. On any given Sunday morning attendees are likely to see mostly women leading worship. Because of this situation of women's leadership, the church has attracted many strong women to its membership and they serve as lay leaders of its activities. Some of them are single women; some are married. More than a few of the married women attend without their husbands. At the same time, the church has a few husbands whose wives attend elsewhere.

I believe it is fair to say, however, that the church has acquired a distinctly female atmosphere in reality as well as in reputation. That is to be expected. Most churches with similar proportions of males in leadership positions would probably have a distinctly male atmosphere. No special reputation would follow it, however, as that would be considered normal. Many women — especially strong women — in a church dominated by male leadership would feel somewhat marginalized even if they could not or would not articulate that. Many of the women at our church left such churches for that reason and joined this one. It is a truly egalitarian church—at least in terms of its self-understanding.

My own observations, based on years of intimate involvement in the life of the church, have led me to believe it is still lacking something. What church isn't? No church is perfect. I love this church better than any other that I know and prefer to worship there and participate in its life in spite of some flaws. What flaws? Well, while the church has achieved the egalitarian dream, it has fallen short of embodying full interdependence. Men and women have full equal rights within the church; no office is closed to either gender and both have equal votes in congregational governance. Every effort is made to achieve a balance of men and women on committees and boards. The fact that four out of seven pastors are women is not due to any conscious design; every open staff position is available equally to qualified men and women candidates.

This church is a beautiful model of the evangelical egalitarians' dream for evangelical church life. However, over the years men have gradually faded into the background while strong women have taken the reigns of leadership. Whose fault is that? I assign no blame. No doubt we men are responsible for the situation; if we stepped up and volunteered more, we would be better represented in leadership positions. Nevertheless, I wonder if liberated women have fully grasped the necessity of gender interdependence in congregational life. Many of them have suffered abuse at the hands of fathers, husbands, brothers, pastors, and bosses. Many of them have struggled mightily to achieve self-esteem and find their own voices as women in a Southern society largely dominated by men. Now they have found a church that honors their femaleness and does not in any way imply that it is inferior to or unequal with maleness. Without adopting a feminist consciousness, some of them have forged ahead in acquiring leadership without considering whether or why men are stepping aside and failing to walk alongside them.

Males and Females Are Different and Interdependent

I believe it is simply a fact of life that men tend to feel threatened by women's success and leadership in organizations. Even those of us who proudly pronounce ourselves fully egalitarian find that somewhere deep inside our masculine egos lies hidden a fear of becoming obsolete or redundant. This has been confirmed for me by Jed Diamond, author of *The Irritable Male Syndrome* (Rodale, 2004), and scholars of other men's studies. Tendency to control situations is a common masculine trait and not just a stereotype (which is not to say some women don't display the same characteristic). Men tend to be goal-oriented and driven and we tend to be individualistic and competitive. There are many exceptions to these generalizations, of course, but these are not mere stereotypes. To those readers who doubt this I recommend books such as *The Essential Difference: The Truth about the Male and Female Brain* by Simon Baron-Cohen of Cambridge University (Basic Books, 2003).

While some scholars continue to argue that gender differences beyond anatomy are exclusively conventional, most contemporary scholarship points to behavioral patterns imprinted on males and females by biology and ontology. Men's and women's brain structures are different and hormones dictate different tendencies without determining behavior exhaustively. From a Christian point of view, male and female differences should be accepted as ontological and not merely biological. God made the genders to complement, not copy, each other. Each has something different to offer the other and both have been affected by the fall into sin in different ways.

I find it interesting that our female-led church has an active and lively women's ministry while lacking any similar men's ministry. In fact, from my point of view, the entire church is a women's ministry. I do not mean that in any negative way. Most churches are one big men's ministry—at least in terms of leadership. Competitive, physical sports play an important role in many churches' congregational lives. They play no role in our church's life. Our church holds a flourishing annual women's retreat attended by nearly one hundred women. No men's retreat or event of any kind has been held in the eight years we have attended. Female participation in "life groups" (what some churches would call "cell churches" or just "small groups") is abundant and active; two of them are for women only. One life group is primarily for men but is poorly attended. Men routinely decline to be nominated as deacons, so the majority of deacons are women.

Don't get me wrong. I'm not blaming the church or its women for any of this. Men have full freedom and ability to organize men's events and lead in congregational life. However, that they do not may signal a lack of complete interdependence between men and women in the church's life. I think this is predictable in any church led so predominantly by women and populated so strongly by strong women. The men tend to fade out of the center and onto the margins. Why? Because neither men nor women have yet fully grasped the importance of male/female interdependence. Just as children need both a mother and a father (studies repeatedly demonstrate that children with involved mothers and fathers flourish more than children with a single parent), so churches need both female and male leaders—both in terms of congregational offices and lay participation.

By no means do I want this brief and admittedly inadequate case study to bias readers against female-led churches. My own membership and participation in this church speak to my belief in the validity of female-led churches. However, I have come to believe that just as male leadership will inevitably lead to at least some women feeling marginalized, so female leadership will inevitably lead to some men feeling left out. In fact, the latter may be a more clearly predictable outcome. Why? Because men are used to leading and, while they may grudgingly accept women's right and ability to lead, they will probably feel neglected and marginalized in a church led by strong women unless the women encourage them to walk alongside them every step of the way.

Women need men just as men need women. A church "for" women is no better than a church "for" men, and it makes no difference whether the situation is intentional or unintended. Women who lead need to acknowledge the unique giftedness of men and not take men for granted just because men have always led and still do lead in most organizations. Nor should Christians argue that neglect of men in a congregation is justified by the ages of male dominance and oppression of women in church and society. Two wrongs never make a right.

Finding Our Way toward Interdependence in Community

Like many nonconservative (I prefer "postconservative") evangelicals I simply take full equality of women and men for granted. It has become a given in my view of the world. I consider subjugation of women to male authority unjust even when women desire and offer it voluntarily. To me, the case for male/female equality in terms of opportunity for power is just as clear as the one for equality of the races. Having lived with that perspective for many years now, I have come to wonder whether it can be a stopping place or whether the next step must be achievement of true interdependence between the genders.

I have gone beyond wondering to concluding that it is so. Men and women are different; about that the complementarians are right. Somehow that traditional insight must be incorporated into the practice of egalitarianism. And just as men need to accept women's differences from themselves as fully valid and necessary for their own full humanity, so women who are enjoying liberation from patriarchy need to realize that their own full humanity depends on healthy relationship with men, including interdependence with them. This means being advocates for males where they are falling behind females in social contexts including education, medical research, health care, and life expectancy.

So what do I suggest for evangelicals who wish to move beyond conservatism into egalitarianism and then into interdependence?

First, egalitarianism is a necessary step toward healthy Christian organizational life. Power must not be concentrated in the hands of any one gender, race, class, or age group. Whenever that is the case, something is wrong. It doesn't matter whether the situation is intentional or not; it should be redressed. If all the deacons or elders are affluent, educated white men, something is amiss. Every effort must be made to include different kinds of people among those with decision-making influence and power.

I oppose enforced quotas because they bind the Holy Spirit. If the Spirit of God wants most of the leaders of a congregation to be men or women or affluent or poor, the Spirit should be free to make it so. However, any evangelical congregation that finds influence and power concentrated in the hands of a group of people too similar to each other should beseech God about his will. They should probably suspect that it is the result of hidden biases rather than God's influence. A healthy congregation will go out of its way to encourage and enable full participation by diverse people. Unity should come from the Spirit, not from human likenesses.

At one business meeting our church found that the entire slate of candidates for a new committee was composed of women. A man dared to stand up and challenge it by saying it did not adequately reflect the makeup of the congregation. The nominating committee responded that they had asked several men to allow their names to be put before the congregation to serve on the committee but that none had responded positively. Still, some men and women felt uncomfortable with having a committee composed solely of one gender. They all knew that in this particular congregation a committee of only men would be regarded as unfair. So, eventually, a couple of good men were found to serve on the new committee. This is as it should be. At least a few good women should also serve on any board or committee alongside men. The same goes for ethnic and racial minorities and for the generational divide. God's gift of diversity needs to be brought out from the margins into the center of every evangelical organization.

My second prescription for achieving interdependence beyond equality, then, is intentionality of diversity on all boards and committees as well as on the staff. But this should not be done out of some sense of political correctness or obligation to fairness; it should be done for the right spiritual reason—our human interdependence. We need to recognize and acknowledge openly that men need women and women need men. They offer distinctive perspectives and styles of relating, decision-making, and governing that should not be silenced or ignored.

A typical man's perspective will be goal-oriented and systematic. A typical woman's perspective will be relational and contextual. Men will typically want clear, predictable processes such as organizational flow charts. Women will typically want collegiality and community. One promotes productivity and accountability; the other promotes peace and inclusion. One seeks closure and progress; the other seeks consensus and harmony. The two do not need to compete; both are valuable ways of leading and decision-making. One without the other will inevitably lead to division or stasis. Healthy life within community depends on both styles being active in Christian leadership of organizations.

Conservative evangelicals tend to emphasize hierarchy in relationships and especially women's submission to the authority of men. Progressive evangelicals have recognized this as unjust and promote full equality of authority and power between women and men in every area of life. But progressive evangelicals have not always fully recognized or acknowledged the truth of complementarianism—a good concept unfortunately hijacked by conservatives to denote their hierarchical view of gender relationships. Males and females are different and their differences complement each other.

Homogeny of the sexes that obliterates these differences is another injustice; the complementary differences should be affirmed as good when kept in check and balanced. Male competitiveness and aggression can get good things accomplished, but they can also become violent. Female nurturing and consensus-building can keep the peace and develop community, but they can also stifle progress in decision-making and goal achievement. The two together, interdependently balancing each other, can cooperate harmoniously to create healthy organizational lives that reflect the full spectrum of vital aspects of the image of God.

TOWARD A POSTCONSERVATIVE EVANGELICALISM

In this book I have attempted to show how it is possible to be more evangelical by being less conservative. I have striven to make clear throughout that being conservative is not always or necessarily bad; in some contexts being conservative is necessary for any evangelical. "Conservative" is a contested concept as is "evangelical." Both have to be defined carefully before anyone knows what is being discussed. In this book, "conservative" has meant a tendency to defend whatever is perceived as traditional and a reluctance to move away from the status quo even under tremendous pressure from new insights, discoveries, and viewpoints provided by experience, including fresh interpretations of the Bible.

"Evangelical" has meant a Christian way of life marked by commitment to the Bible as God's authoritative Word transcending traditions, belief in conversion as the only entrance into authentic Christian life, devotion centered on the cross of Jesus Christ as the only means of salvation for humanity, and activism in evangelism, missions, and social transformation. It has also here meant respect for the Great Tradition of Christian doctrinal teaching, including especially the insights of the church fathers and Reformers even when aspects of that tradition must be judged mistaken in the light of Scripture.

My concern is that contemporary evangelical life is too conservative to be fully and authentically evangelical. To me, being evangelical means taking risks with regard to change and being radical with regard to human traditions—especially those that are bound to culture and shaped by human vested interests. "Radical" means "going back to the roots," and the roots we must go back to are Jesus Christ, the apostles, the Bible, and our own callings out of self-enclosed darkness into God's marvelous light. Being evangelical should be a journey backward and forward and never a static settlement into one location; it should always include reconsideration of traditional positions especially insofar as they are humanly devised to protect and defend a status quo.

Evangelicals often are too concerned with "being conservative," and not only in contrast to real religious liberalism, which is not the least interesting to me. Too often being conservative as an evangelical means having a fortress mentality that shuts out new facts and realities and defending traditional beliefs and practices for no other reason than that they are conventional.

Also, it is unfortunate that "evangelical" has come to be equated with the Religious Right in American social and political life whereas, in fact, evangelicals have often in the past been social and political progressives. Too many media pundits and journalists simply equate "evangelical" with "social and political conservatism." Many of us who have sound evangelical pedigrees and warmly embrace evangelical beliefs and practices resist this popular equation because we also regard ourselves as social and political progressives. There is no conflict between these two commitments. In fact, many of us believe they imply each other; we are social and political progressives because we are evangelicals and we are evangelicals, in part at least, because we are social and political progressives.

How does that work? Well, we find the only sound basis for our humanism in the Christian doctrine of humanity in the image of God. Without a personal, caring God in whose image all people are created, there is no objective foundation for caring for the welfare of all people. Without that vision of God there is no objective foundation for caring for the nonhuman environment. Our social and political progressivism is rooted in the soil of our evangelical faith. This may seem counterintuitive to secularists and religious conservatives, but it makes perfect sense to us. We believe the only reason for that situation is the popular misconception, especially in the media, of all evangelicals as necessarily conservative.

What I propose in this book and others is that progressive evangelicals move beyond conservatism into what I call "post-conservative evangelicalism" *rather than* drop the label "evangelical" altogether (as some have done). Being evangelical is simply too much a part of my identity (and I know many others who share this self-understanding) to become what has been termed "postevangelical." But I am not committed to being conservative in the same way. I am conservative in some situations (such as among real theological liberals or secular humanists) but not among evangelicals. I am not alone; many of my evangelical friends and acquaintances are also embarrassed to be called evangelicals because of the popular identification of that label with social and political conservatism as well as with Christian fundamentalism.

When I am asked what kind of evangelical I am, I say "post-conservative." Many people do not yet understand what that means, but it's not hard to explain. I simply respond to their quizzical expressions with "I'm a God-fearing, Bible-believing, Jesus-loving Christian who believes religious traditions are always open to reform in the light of God's Word." I often say something to distance myself from the Religious Right, such as "I believe if Jesus were here today he would identify with the poor and oppressed more than with the wealthy and powerful." My hope is that other evangelicals like myself will hold onto their evangelical identity and not allow it to be hijacked by social and political conservatives and religious traditionalists.

Questions to All Your Answers

The Journey from Folk Religion to Examined Faith

Roger E. Olson

"Jesus is the answer."
"God has a perfect plan for your life."
"All sins are equal."

Sayings like these may make catchy bumper stickers, but as deep, life-changing truths they fall short. They are the earmarks of "folk religion"—a badly distorted pop-Christianity that thrives on clichés and slogans and resists reflection and examination. Such pat spiritual answers often contain a nugget of truth, but that truth is easily misunderstood and misapplied in ways that do more harm than good.

Roger Olson encourages us to reach for a higher and deeper faith. Examining ten prevalent Christian beliefs, he raises questions that encourage us to engage our minds with the Scriptures in order to carefully consider what it is we believe and why. You'll be surprised at what you find. *Questions to All Your Answers* will help you use the God-given gift of your intellect to sift through glib sayings that sound right to what actually is right—to truth that really can set you and others free.

Hardcover, Jacketed: 0-310-27336-6

Pick up a copy today at your favorite bookstore!

ZONDERVAN®
.com

We want to hear from you. Please send your comments about this book to us in care of zreview@zondervan.com. Thank you.

ZONDERVAN.com/
AUTHORTRACKER
follow your favorite authors